Starting Over

Starting Over

25 Rules When You've Bottomed Out

By Mary Lee Gannon

New Horizon Press
Far Hills, New Jersey

New Horizon Press
P.O. Box 669
Far Hills, NJ 07931

Gannon, Mary Lee
Starting Over: 25 Rules When You've Bottomed Out

Cover design: Robert Aulicino
Interior design: Susan Sanderson

Library of Congress Control Number: 2009922796

ISBN 13: 978-0-88282-311-9
New Horizon Press

Manufactured in the U.S.A.

2014   2013   2012   2011   2010   /   5   4   3   2   1

This book is dedicated to Maria, Brianna, Andrea and Max.

You are my heroes.

Author's Note

This book is based on extensive interviews as well as the personal experiences and insights of the author and the subjects who complied with appearing in its pages. Some names have been changed in order to protect privacy except for those of contributing experts.

Acknowledgments

I want to acknowledge all the people who opened doors, mentored and advised me, listened and nurtured my soul along the way—too many to list here. Some of these special guides include: Len Barcousky for guiding me as a reporter at the *Pittsburgh Post-Gazette*; Roger Friday for teaching me the art of sales; the Board of Directors of Three Rivers Advertising Specialty Association for empowering my innovation to create a new strategy; Jack Connors for teaching me the art of networking and fundraising; Bill Provenzano at Ohio Valley General Hospital for allowing me the leverage to grow in my first role as a full-time fundraiser; the Board of Directors of Forbes Health Foundation for supporting my lead like family; the Pittsburgh Society of Association Executives for underscoring leadership; Diane Frndak for suggesting that I write this book; my parents from whom I learned character and integrity at a very young age and my countless friends, who have been a source of inspiration and support every step of the way.

Table of Contents

Foreword

My story is living testament that anyone can turn his or her life around. At thirty-five years old, I was a stay-at-home mother with four children under seven years old and a self-employed husband. I had a two-year allied health degree at which I had been earning an average salary when I left the workforce to be a full-time mother. My marriage had become intolerable and I filed for divorce. A few months later, I was deluged by an overwhelming avalanche of litigation and anger that resulted in the children and me going from residing in the most exclusive suburb of Pittsburgh to being homeless, carless and hungry. We went from the country club life to losing our home and becoming poverty stricken all within a short span of time.

What I have come to realize over the years following this time of despair is that people can only take away your things but they can't take away your spirit, which is something you control. If you choose to allow others to take away your peace, your sense of humor, your ability to love and nurture and your integrity, then you have begun to value what the evil hold dear: power, money and material goods. Nobody said that the one holding the most stuff gets the most peace. Have you ever noticed that sometimes those who value "stuff" tend to be manipulative? Could it be because all of the trappings do not settle a soul?

The desire to acquire "stuff" can never be satisfied. There will always be more stuff to acquire. It is human nature to cling to and protect the things that you feel are yours. However, the true essence of who you are is not defined by the *things* around you. It is defined by the *people* around you—the people you value and the people who value you. It is realized by the emotion in your heart.

In times of great personal challenge, you realize very quickly what is truly important in life. You must draw on your strengths, convert your weaknesses and give thanks for the blessings around you. My children and I are grateful that we live in a country which has afforded us the ability to have survived on welfare, food stamps and medical assistance. We are grateful for the lessons we learned through this challenge that delivered us from relying on public assistance to self-sufficiency and then abundance. We are grateful for the people who guided us and mentored us along the way. It has contributed to who we are today. This book is my chance to give back, in some small way, advice, strategies and steps to recovery that have helped me and may help others who are engaged in a life transition or those who are simply seeking strategies for success.

Very early in our family's struggles, I realized that I was going to be the one to provide for my children and had to figure out a way to do so quickly. Choosing to be a full-time mother, I hadn't worked outside the home in seven years. I was faced with crisis management. However, while at home, I had done a lot of writing for organizations in which I had volunteered and decided to send clips of that writing to the largest local metropolitan newspaper in our city. Much to my surprise, they hired me as a freelance reporter and I began to write for a number of other magazines, news and professional publications. From there, I earned a certification as an association management executive and went on to be a self-employed public relations consultant, business writer and trade association executive director, all work I did from home. People ask me where I got my confidence to apply for positions in which I had little to no experience. I tell them it was because I never doubted that I could learn just about anything and I was willing to do whatever it took to meet the needs of my children.

Public assistance was not the way I wanted to live my life. I did the big cry and a lot of asking, "Why me?" but that got me nothing but more paralyzed with fear.

I needed adequate health benefits for the children and myself after the divorce, so I decided to enter the corporate world. I taught myself how to network, write grant proposals and desktop publish, among other skills, and then went on to be the executive director of a hospital foundation. Today I am the president and CEO of a large hospital foundation, I have owned my own home for several years and my three oldest children are in excellent colleges—something I never thought I would be able to afford—and my son is achieving well in high school as he gets ready for college.

I teach classes at a local college and volunteer at community organizations to help others make life transitions that will bring them greater personal and financial reward. In this book, I focus on the foundation I live by in achieving what I set out to do and what I convey to my students and those whom I mentor.

You will also read testimonials from other individuals who have overcome great challenges to achieve personal and professional success. Some are employed in the corporate world and some are self-employed. They range in education from high school graduates to those with their Ph.D. The measures of their financial success vary and are not related to their education. All have conquered great trials to achieve autonomy in their work and personal peace in their lives. I was astounded at how similar their mind-sets are to one another and to mine. As you read their stories, you will find two common themes:

1. They are fearless, not reckless.
2. They figure things out or ask for help.

If I can come back from overwhelming adversity, anyone can. I know you can, too. I will show you how to harness your own resources. You already have everything you need. Additionally, the chapter exercises and worksheets at the end of each chapter will give you a concrete "Personal Development Plan" to chart your new course.

Introduction

Okay, so you want to make some changes in your life, but those changes scare you a little, invigorate you a lot and the ambivalence sometimes paralyzes you. You just don't know if you can make it work but you know you have the energy to make a difference. What you don't realize is that you have already been through this before and succeeded. This book will show you how to put those strategies to work again. Make notes in the margins, because when you finish reading it and doing the exercises, you will have a definitive map to move forward. This book is direct and to the point so that you don't spend a lot of time reading and can get on to making things happen for yourself.

Remember the first day of school, the first day of scouts, the first day at camp, team tryouts, going away to college and starting a new job? You weren't sure if people would like you or your book bag. You couldn't count on getting played with a lot in every game. You didn't know if the lonely feeling of standing out would make way for reward.

How you met these challenges head-on is exactly how you will overcome any new challenge. First you taught yourself how to accept the situation. And once you learned to cope, you strategized for better success. Acceptance comes first so that your emotions aren't in the way when you need to plan, as planning is imperative for success. This book will give you that plan.

Life is a little bit like the popular family game *Chutes and Ladders*. This game is timeless and appeals to people of all ages because of one simple fact: Anyone can win! The game does not require any logic or strategy—just luck. Preschoolers can beat their parents. Grandma, who has never played before, can beat the bully on the block on any given day. Players learn to follow basic rules, take turns and play cooperatively—all skills that aid anyone in life. Life is sometimes like *Chutes and Ladders*—sometimes it appears that others have all the luck.

Chutes and Ladders began in ancient India, where it was used to teach Hindu children about right and wrong. The bases of the ladders stood on squares that symbolized different types of good and then there were slippery snakes that snuck out from squares representing various types of evil. The literal usage of the good vs. bad paradigm caught Victorian England's fancy, and in the late nineteenth century, the game was played throughout the United Kingdom. It was called *Snakes and Ladders*, and very Victorian virtues like penitence, thrift and industry were the elements that shot a player up the ladders. The *Chutes and Ladders* we know today was copyrighted in 1870 and came to the United States thereafter.

In our childhood, *Chutes and Ladders* taught us a lot about coping with adversity that is beyond our control. The game contains twists and turns and the potential for good and bad surprises. Because the results of the spinning arrow are completely random, progress through the tiers is luck-based, evening the odds for everyone. Players move to squares that contain examples of good or bad deeds: Save a cat from a tree, climb a ladder. Eat too much candy or engage in scary bicycle antics, get ready to plummet. The only safe thing to bet on is that the lessons will keep coming and coming, which is a lot like life. Players have an opportunity to learn good sportsmanship, as they may gain or lose extra ground suddenly to circumstances that they cannot control. A player may be rows ahead of other competitors, only to land on a chute and have to slide back to the bottom row.

There is no strategy here, no way to cheat, no way to outsmart opponents with slippery head games or a convincing poker face.

If you enjoy *Chutes and Ladders*, you've accepted that there are some things over which you have no control. You enjoy the ride with all of its turns. If the game frustrates you, then you haven't quite got to the acceptance point. But life is more than defining and accepting things out of our control. What is the next step?

The next step is what *Starting Over* will show you—how to get old habits out of the way so that you can create a plan that will bring you happiness and fulfillment.

Let's look at a scenario you may find familiar.

Meredith and Jessica are third graders who are standing in line at the bus stop.

Charlie shows up and cuts in front of them just before the bus opens its doors. He scales the steps two at a time and beats them to the last seat on the bus where the girls have sat every day since school began. Charlie throws his elbows up over the seat in front of him.

"Got your seat!" he sneers, leaning forward with a Cheshire cat grin.

Meredith stands up straight and announces, "Bus driver! Charlie Mauro just stole our seat." She stomps her feet walking to the back of the bus, pointing at Charlie. "He cut in front of us in line and should go to the principal's office."

Jessica watches the bus driver sip his coffee from a shop that charges more for coffee than the price of her lunch. She slides into the seat in front of Charlie. "Meredith, let's just sit here today."

"No way! That is *our* seat."

More children file onto the bus before it starts to pull away from the curb.

Meredith is jostled down into the seat next to Jessica and lets out a sigh that would have put the big bad wolf to shame. "I hate that Charlie Mauro and I am going to tell his homeroom teacher what he did as soon as we get to school."

He pokes his face between them and bellows, "I'm so scaaaaaared."

Meredith starts twisting the key tags on her backpack until one breaks off.

Jessica opens her backpack and starts flipping through her flash cards. There is a spelling test first period and she kept getting the word "consume" wrong last night when she was practicing.

Who Do You Want To Be?

Meredith is not able to accept or control the situation—she is heading down a *chute*. Charlie is controlling the situation playing his own game. The bus driver is disinterested in the situation—he quit the game early. Meanwhile, Jessica chooses not to let having to change seats get in the way of what she needs to do—study for the test. She is the only person on a *ladder.*

Jessica realizes that the energy spent on fighting for a certain seat on the bus does not have anything to do with where she ultimately wants to be. She wants to get an "A" on the spelling test. Meredith probably wants that, too. However, fighting with Charlie is easier and probably fulfills an emotional need that she harbors to either control or to be heard. Either way, fulfilling this emotional need is not going to get her an "A" on the spelling test.

It is very easy to get distracted from your goals with emotions that really do not have anything to do with where you want to be. People do this, because it is easier than focusing on something that is more intimidating—owning your own accomplishments. You can fail at reaching goals. You can't fail at arguing. Anger is easier.

Know the difference between your emotions and your goals. Get the *chutes* of your own negative emotions out of the way so that you can climb up the *ladders* to success.

Make sure that what you are pursuing is a *career* and not a *job*. There is a distinct difference. That career might be starting your own business or it might be building a skill set that will equip you for a higher management position. Your job is what you are doing today; your career is the trajectory of your working life's achievements to make a difference in people's lives. It's the journey that makes you a "must have" member of any team. If the job you are doing today does not further you on your journey, it is time to look for another opportunity. That opportunity should be a career building choice.

A job is simply something you are currently doing to earn money and does not offer a lot of networking opportunities. A career is a series of connected employment and networking opportunities, where you build up skills to move you into higher paying and higher prestige employment opportunities later on. Most people do not stay with companies throughout their entire careers as they did twenty years ago. Chances are the job you are doing today is not anything like what you will be doing in five years. If you find that after a year you are still doing the same work that you were doing a year ago without opportunities to develop a broader set of skills or network with other professionals, you may be in a dead-end job.

If your employment situation seems more like a job than a career, consider other opportunities. If there is no room for advancement where you are currently employed, you should look elsewhere. You want to be in a position to receive a promotion. Conserve your energy to build your career development experience. You will want to be in a position where you can meet new people and develop relationships that will broaden your sphere of influence. You want to make an impression that will be noticed.

Are you making the most of your current position? Consider two young people who take jobs lifeguarding at their local community pool. Lifeguarding might seem like a fairly predictable job. Michelle shows up on time, works her shift and when her shift is over, does her closing tasks and goes home. Clayton shows up ten minutes early, picks up some trash around the pool deck, works his shift, asks the manager on his break if there is anything that needs to be done, does his closing tasks and sticks around fifteen minutes later to talk with the other guards and give a break to a snack bar employee who had worked an extra three hours. Who do you think will be considered for the assistant manager position next year?

Use this book as a resource to make steps toward your new destination. Read it through and then reference it when you need advice on a particular topic or when you are stuck and just not sure what to do next. Use a highlighter to emphasize what is significant to you. Most importantly, in choosing *Starting Over*, know that you are ready and willing to make different decisions for the future. Bravo! That is the only way that change occurs.

Chapter One

Rule No. 1

Begin with a "Success Sketch" and Hang It Where You Will See It Every Day

Human nature tells you to make a plan from the beginning. Start with the end in mind, draw what that will look like on paper and post your "Success Sketch" where you can see it every day. Stick people are acceptable! You won't forget where you are headed if you have to look at this sketch every day. When you get mired down in the trivial nature of everyday routines, this will remind you that you have a bigger picture in mind.

If you are changing jobs, don't blindly answer classified ads and send out résumés. Begin by making sure you want to stay in the same profession. If not, then read up on career choices that interest you and in which you have transferable skills. Sketch yourself in your new role, smiling, being happy in your new office, house or when meeting and greeting potential customers.

I have an index card with my "Success Sketch" posted above my desk in my bedroom. On the back of a lined index card is a pencil drawn picture of myself advising students in my class on career advice while other allied professionals offer helpful advice nearby.

For instance, if you are looking for a new home, don't start by determining the price you can afford, start with numbering the priorities of what you ultimately want:

1. Proximity to work
2. School district
3. Proximity to shopping

4. Number of bedrooms
5. Family room on first floor

Picture yourself living there—actually walking around the house and getting in the car to go to work in the morning. Draw that house on a diagram with your office and schools and post it where you will see it every day. If you are leaving home or starting a new life, where do you ultimately want to end up? I suspect that it isn't in a one-bedroom apartment in a questionable part of town. Perhaps you want to have a small home in a nice neighborhood.

When you have the answer to what your ultimate goal is, share this with a mentor who will help you form the path to your vision. Life isn't simply about getting through the day to get onto the next. It is about making the world a better place for those around us, so that we may live in peace and joy with the ones we love. How can you get to where you really want to be if you do not know where that is?

When you have in mind what you ultimately want to achieve, the path to getting there will become clearer. The path to success is foggy only when what you want is foggy. The end result must be clear in your mind.

You may want to start a business but do not know what kind of business would be right for you. If this is true, start reading the classified advertisements for business opportunities. Perhaps you'll see a vending machine business that has a low cost of entry and—Boom!—you buy it and become a business owner. Then you realize that vending machines are heavy and need to be transported and you do not have a truck. This business requires a lot of time on the road and you do not like to drive. And the business is more competitive than you thought, because anyone can purchase the machines. It's locating them and having a good agreement with vendors that is crucial to success.

If you had begun with the end in mind you may have started by visualizing what your desired ultimate workday would be like:

1. Small office in or close to your home
2. Few or no employees
3. Low overhead
4. Little to no travel
5. Using your multitasking ability

As you start to frame these priorities, specific examples of lines of work will come to mind. Low overhead generally lends itself to service related work such as writing, design, temporary staffing, cleaning agency or consulting. If you had wanted to do something creative that could grow into something bigger, you may be a seamstress who designs coats that can be mass-produced in China or a designer of jewelry made from sea glass.

If you are not sure what you specifically want to do, sketch yourself in your ideal work environment and post it in your home office, bedroom or kitchen. As the vision becomes clearer, you can draw in the particulars.

Rule Break: *(Every section holds a "Rule Break" designed to challenge you to think about things in a nontraditional manner. Diverting from what is common and obvious usually stands out and gets noticed.)* Instead of thinking about the things that worry you, start repeatedly seeing yourself at the END of your dream—not all that you are going to go through to get there, but what it will feel like to be THERE! Say to yourself every day, "I will be_____(a corporate executive, living at the beach, enjoying the love of my life)." Make no room in your head for anything outside of that vision. If other thoughts creep in, repeat your mantra out loud.

Ten Key Questions to Begin with the End in Mind:
1. *Where do you want to live?* Current neighborhood? In the city? In the country? At the beach?
2. *Where do you want to work?* Home? Small office? Large corporation? Close to home? Doesn't matter? Don't want to work?
3. *Do you like to plan things systematically or are you creative and free-flowing?*
4. *Do you want to take direction or give direction?*
5. *Do you value flexibility in your schedule?*
6. *Do you like to work on one task at a time or do you prefer multitasking?*
7. *Do you like to travel during a typical day or prefer to work in a set location? A mix?*
8. *Do you want to work/live with a lot of people around you or a few?*
9. *What qualities do you see in successful people?* Are you cultivating those?
10. *Do you mark your calendar so that every two months you monitor your progress, changing, adding or editing your sketch if necessary?*

Kellyann's Story
At the age of thirty, Kellyann Dinoff had her dream job. She was a marketing manager for a market-leading technology company. She had absolute

autonomy, a top salary and worked with great people. Then the technology bubble burst, greatness crashed to despair and Kellyann found herself among the ranks of the unemployed.

With a determined attitude, she began her search for a new job only to discover that her challenges were mounting. A week after being laid off, she found out that she was pregnant. It was a joyous occasion for Kellyann and her husband, but realistically she knew it made her mission for employment questionable. Now she had to find a job while trying to disguise her pregnancy. As her belly grew, her job prospects dwindled. Kellyann recalls "resigning" herself to taking independent contract work to supplement income, vowing to start her job search again once her baby was six months old.

Seven months after the birth of her daughter, Kellyann resumed job hunting and was contacted by a former colleague who was launching a company. He needed a marketing director, but could not employ her full time. She again "resigned" herself to taking contract work while still not interested in being self-employed. Kellyan felt owning her own business was more than she could handle, that the chances of success were slim while the risks and investment of time and money were great. She just wanted to work and collect a paycheck even though the longest she had ever held an employed position was two and a half years and she had been laid off from every job she ever had. Still, she was searching for her next "dream job."

In the meantime, more contract work kept coming her way. The realtor who sold her and her husband their house needed help marketing a new development, so Kellyann designed ads and created marketing materials for her. She helped friends develop plans and strategies for marketing their new businesses. Prospects of full-time employment had been few and far between, as only positions demanding long and unpredictable hours with frequent travel were available—not conducive to a new family. Still, Kellyann was not interested in being self-employed. The right job was out there and she would find it.

Seven years later, Kellyann had yet to find full-time employment. Instead, she had acquired a steady stream of interesting projects that continually led to more and more contract work. She was filling a need in the business world that could not be met with full-time employees, who were much more costly than contracted short-term work.

"I was working less hours than I had at my 'real' job, was healthier, happier and earning good money," remembers Kellyann. "It dawned on me finally that I had found a new job—my dream job—as a business owner."

Kellyann's husband, a successful entrepreneur himself, became a mentor in helping to establish herself as an independent contractor, eventually incorporating in 2007 as Sonance Communications, a boutique marketing communications agency.

"I stumbled into my dream job in this accidental business," admits Kellyann, whose business recently grew by 50 percent. "I have more freedom, satisfaction and security than I ever had in my 'secure' corporate positions."

The only thing Kellyann wishes is that she would have realized earlier that she was in business for herself for the long haul. She would have started marketing herself as a company rather than an individual much earlier.

"Had I done this, I believe my business would be even bigger than it is now."

Kellyann has created a network of colleagues that want a better balance of work and personal life.

"Many of the contractors I hire are women like myself who have left the workforce and do not want to go back to fifty- to sixty-hour-a-week jobs," she said. "And we are all doing the things we like to do while having control over our own destinies."

Remember: Begin with the end in mind and post your "Success Sketch" where you can see it. Think about the things that are important to you. Family time? Close proximity to work? Work that you love? Flexibility? Predictability? Don't just look to find "a job." Craft your own destiny based on where you ultimately want to be.

Exercise #1
From Rule No. 1: Begin with a "Success Sketch" and Hang It Where You Will See It Every Day

Begin with the End in Mind and Sketch That Vision on Paper

Ten Key Questions:
1. Where do you want to live? Current neighborhood? In the city? In the country? At the beach?

2. Where do you want to work? Home? Small office? Large corporation? Close to home? Doesn't matter? Don't want to work?

3. Do you like to plan things systematically or are you creative and free-flowing?

4. Do you want to take direction or give direction?

5. Do you value flexibility in your schedule?

6. Do you like to work on one task at a time or do you prefer multitasking?

7. Do you like to travel during a typical day or prefer to stay at home or in the office? A mix?

8. Do you want to work/live with a lot of people around you or a few?

9. What qualities do you see in successful people? Are you cultivating those?

10. Mark your calendar so that every two months you monitor your progress. Change, add to or edit your sketch if necessary.

Exercise #1a
From Rule No. 1: Begin with a "Success Sketch"
and Hang It Where You Will See It Every Day

"My Success Sketch"

This sketch shows me doing what I ultimately want to do and reflects my answers to the questions under rule 1.

Exercise #1b
From Rule No. 1: Begin with a "Success Sketch" and Hang It
Where You Will See It Every Day

Write Your Retirement Speech Now—
How Do You Want to Be Remembered?

If you really want to start with the end in mind, write your retirement speech now. This exercise will show you where you want to be at the end of your career. It is your job to work on a life plan that will get you there. This book will help you with that. But for now, think about what it will be like at the end of your career when all of your friends and family are gathered together to celebrate your accomplishments and you are called to the podium to make a speech.

1. What would be the first thing you would say?
2. Who would you thank for supporting you along the way?
3. Who would you acknowledge and what did they teach you?
4. Of everything you have worked on, what was the most important?
5. What was the most valuable lesson you learned?

Chapter Two

Rule No. 2

Find a Mentor in an Offbeat Place

The wonderful thing about taking on a new challenge at any point in your life is that there is no end to what you may accomplish. Reading this book shows that you have the energy to do something different in your life and that you are seeking guidance on how to do just that. However, energy is not enough. Guidance is critical to help you chart a path and stay on it, especially when it comes from a trusted source who has been through challenges and persevered. I believe this guidance is necessary to help you stay the course during tough times. It will help you so that you don't wander over to the same dreary path you have traveled before. Habits are hard to break. Mentors will be able to look objectively at your progress and offer a fresh perspective without the bias of your past experiences.

We are all creatures of habit. Not because we are bad people, but human beings are comforted by continuity. This is why so many people stay in unhappy jobs and in unhealthy relationships. It takes a lot more courage to leave what is familiar, no matter how discouraging it is, and to venture into uncharted territory. Fear of the same seems to carry less risk than fear of the unknown. A place you have never been may not be safe. You feel safe in what you know, no matter how desperate, because it is predictable.

The problem with staying with something predictable is that it may become a deterrent to your happiness if it is not productive or healthy for you. If you have been in a bad job or a bad relationship for a while, your self-confidence has been depleted. Your sense of normalcy has crept lower with each day so that you wind up doubting yourself, not seeing a brighter future and figuring that you might as well just accept your situation, because it has become "normal" to you. In a way, you forget who you are and submit to being a bystander in your own life.

But you don't want to feel that way today or you would not be seeking a new direction for your life by reading this book. So why take a new journey with the same map if you want to end up in a different destination? Find a mentor: a wise and trustworthy counselor or teacher who has vast life experience and is reflective and supportive.

How do you find good mentors? Once you know what it is that you want to achieve (and that may come in little steps), seek a mentor who has already accomplished something similar. You will have a lot of mentors in your life. As your goals change, so may your mentors. A mentor will help you, because s/he sees in you the ideals and dedication that it will take to succeed. Mentors will see a little of their own spirit in you. If they like you, they will want to see you succeed and will want to be a part of that success.

12-step programs like Alcoholics Anonymous, Gamblers Anonymous and Al-Anon, which address life's most devastating habits, are designed with mentors called "sponsors" for this same reason. A mentor has been through challenges and knows the temptations that occur especially when times are bad. A mentor will keep you from making the same mistakes you may have made before, because they know the pitfalls that come from taking the easy shortcut that often ends up being a painful, long-term voyage. They may become the best professional (and possibly personal) friend you will ever have.

If you are starting a business, find a mentor who has started a similar business. If you are writing a book, seek a mentor who has done so. If you are seeking to become a manager, look for other managers who will mentor you. Search for mentors who have not had it easy. Seek those who have mounted insurmountable odds.

When I was faced with becoming the primary source of income for my four children, I took an inventory of my skills, assessed what lines of work would give me the greatest financial return knowing my talents and charted a course that would build those talents. Mentors were vitally important in helping me to learn what I didn't know and what I couldn't read in a book, including how to negotiate when the deal was failing, how to break into a conversation that was otherwise closed and how to engage and motivate people among other valuable insights.

I began my new career path with my love and basic skill of writing. I had done a lot of writing for volunteer organizations when I was a stay-at-home mother and sent clips of my writing to the *Pittsburgh Post-Gazette*, my area's largest local metropolitan newspaper. I was hired to be a freelance reporter. I did not have a journalism degree nor had I ever written for a newspaper. As a matter of fact, I only had a two-year degree in an allied health field at which I was making an average salary when I left it to become a full-time mom. I joined a writer's group of other *Post-Gazette* freelance writers so that I could mentor under them on how they addressed issues inherent to reporting. I suppose I could have found a famous writer in Pittsburgh to mentor me, but I learned more from my freelance colleagues than I could have ever hoped to learn from anyone. One of those colleagues recommended me for a part-time position as public relations director of a public school district where she was a school board member. I was able to secure that position, allowing me the freedom to work at home.

I joined several writers' groups at the time to help improve my craft. I had previously done some writing for children, which taught me to write tightly by saying a lot in a few words. This skill transferred well to newspaper writing where every word could otherwise be used for advertising space. I was beginning to understand that everything I was going through was for a reason—a lesson per se. I became a student who was thirsty to learn more.

I never was defensive when my newspaper stories were edited; I considered editing a learning experience. To have the best educated editors at an award-winning newspaper critique my writing were gifts that I treasured. The editors only had to tell me something once. I never argued with them and tried to be a very quick study. I was fortunate enough to land more assignments from the *Post-Gazette* and other publications than I could keep up with. I attribute my writing skills today to what I learned from my editors and mentors while with the *Pittsburgh Post-Gazette*.

Yet as much as I valued developing my writing abilities, I knew I needed to diversify my skills in order to acquire more work. So I pursued work in the affiliated fields of public relations and business communications. I was grateful to have many clients and mentors during this time.

I discovered quickly that freelance work was not going to afford me the living that was needed to support five people. I did not have employment benefits for the children's or my healthcare, dental and vision needs. So I assessed my ability to lead and talk to people and decided to build up my sales skills.

I had a wonderful mentor in the advertising specialty industry who allowed me to follow him around on sales calls. It was there that I learned the art of selling and that the best price did not always get the sale. The best service and the best relationship sealed the deal. I could see that people in sales who were good at what they did had the ability to move into higher paying positions in a variety of companies. I like people, and to hear a person say "no" to something I was pitching was not the worst thing that had ever happened to me. So I became resilient and took every opposition as a learning experience. I could see that people with strong sales skills, for the most part, were making more than those with strong writing skills. But the field of sales is extremely competitive. So I decided to transfer those skills into a field that needed strong people and motivational skills but drew far less competition than sales. For me, that field was fundraising. Most people would be comfortable trying to sell you something before they would feel comfortable asking you for money. But I could see the good work that fundraising provided the community. As a young girl, I had mentored under my mother in a number of volunteer fundraising activities that ranged from helping blind people adjust to society to providing food for the hungry to creating improvements in our church and schools, just to name a few. I knew that professional fundraising was not just an art, but had a science to it as well. So I purchased books on the subject at the bookstore and borrowed books from the library to study that science.

While working at the newspaper and as the freelance public relations director of the public school district, members of that school board became some of the best mentors in fundraising I have ever seen. I never formally asked them to mentor me; I simply observed. More on that experience is featured in a later chapter.

Rule Break: Some may think that a mentor should be a very successful, high profile individual. I suggest that you not look in that direction. The president of a company or a highly recognized leader may be too busy to take a personal interest in YOU. Try to find someone who has a lower profile, quietly achieved the same objectives, turned his or her life around and wants to make time for you.

How to Find a Mentor for YOU:
1. *Find someone with a similar history.* Look for someone who has done what you want to accomplish, maybe not on the grandest scale, but who has consistently succeeded with innumerable challenges. Look

for this person in a company similar to yours but is not a competitor. Look at professional organizations, where people with your similar goals meet to share ideas and grow. Also look in nontraditional places: your church, book group, local pool or gym. If you are seeking guidance on starting a business, someone at one of the governmental agencies, such as the Small Business Administration (SBA) or Service Core of Retired Executives (SCORE), may be helpful. Look in the phone book for similar businesses in another part of town with which you would not be in competition. Also, ask friends if they know someone who has done what you want to accomplish.

2. *Find someone who is interested in helping you.* The person living the greatest success story in the world will not afford anything for you if he or she does not have time to meet with you and guide you. Spend time talking with potential mentors to find the right fit.

3. *Look online for similar stories.* Someone in another city may be available to help you via the Internet but this does not substitute for someone with whom you can meet face-to-face. People in other cities, though, may not be as fearful that you will be a competitor of theirs.

4. *Set up a lunch with a potential mentor.* Generally this will be someone whom you have already met and about whom you have a good feeling. If there is someone you have identified as a good potential mentor and you run into him or her at a social or professional gathering, introduce yourself and share your admiration of the person's success. It is often worthwhile to find a mentor within a company in which you already work or may be seeking to work. Ask specific questions about how the person got to where he or she is— questions that let the individual know you are aware of specific information about his or her company. Questions such as:

*   How did you get started in the field?
*   What do you like most/least about your work?
*   What is your typical day like?
*   What emerging trends do you see affecting your industry in the next five years?
*   What skill sets and abilities will I need to be successful in this line of work?

People are always flattered by your interest in their stories. If you feel the connection is good, ask if you may follow up with a call to take him or her to lunch to continue the discussion of that person's success. If there seems to be a good fit between you at lunch, ask if you may meet with him or her occasionally so that you can gain insight from the person's experiences. Tell the person that you admire his or her accomplishments and that you would really like to be able to follow in the person's blueprint of success. Most likely, that person will be flattered. Ask if he or she would be interested in mentoring you. Lunch is always your treat. Come prepared with specific examples of what you are doing toward your goal. Sometimes I have "quiet mentors" who are people I take to lunch or meet several times a year, but I do not formalize the process by asking them to be mentors. We just enjoy spending time together, advising each other and building a lifelong friendship. Friends want to help friends. Relationships are the source of happiness and success.

5. *Send creative instruments of gratitude often.* If people do something nice for you, you can never thank them enough. Send your mentor a card on Boss's Day that may say, "I know you are not my boss, but you have been a valued teacher and trusted example of success in my life." Send an interesting book that you think he or she would enjoy. Ask what his or her birthday is and have flowers or a fruit basket delivered on that day. Send a homemade treat at Thanksgiving with a note that expresses your gratitude.

Once you have experienced the value of a mentor, don't forget what it meant to you. Offer to mentor someone else. The experience of mentoring helps you to give back a little of what you have been granted. In doing so, you will learn something new about yourself and nurture a fresh voice in the business world.

Victoria's Story

Victoria was thirty years old and selling advertising for a local radio station in the ski town of Sun Valley, Idaho. The only competition she had was newspaper advertising. Her clients repeatedly asked her how they could better reach the visitors who were not making time to read the local newspaper on their ski trips. It wasn't until she and a girlfriend went on a getaway weekend to Aspen, Colorado, that she came up with a solution to her clients' problem.

Once the women had arrived at their Aspen hotel and checked in at the front desk, they were handed an illustrated map with advertisements around the perimeter. This map served as an immediate resource for the selection of their first restaurant and continued to help them chart activities for the rest of their stay.

"Within twenty minutes I had made my first buying decision," said Victoria. "That map was exactly what my clients were looking for."

Victoria researched what it would cost to illustrate and print a similar map for Sun City. Then she invested her life's savings of $1,000 and set fees for what to charge the advertisers. Suddenly she was moonlighting in her own business.

Asking questions of knowledgeable people was a big part of what Victoria did correctly from the start. She remembers being silent and truly listening to the advice she was given.

"Successful people have one thing in common," said Victoria. "They know to leave their egos at the door and become completely teachable. I knew I didn't know anything and was excited to learn. I was like a sponge."

Faced with the challenge of quitting her radio job to take on her business full time, Victoria decided to expand her venture into a new market 500 miles, four remote mountain passes and many snowstorms away. She ultimately quit her job, left her two small children with her husband and departed home for ten weeks, as it was too far to commute and they did not have the money to fly back and forth for visits. In a viral snowstorm she kissed her family goodbye and got on the road.

"Something inside me told me this was going to be one of the most important decisions of my life," observed Victoria.

Sixty miles from home Victoria's car went into a 360-degree spin, hit a guardrail and came to a screeching halt on the downturn of a steep mountain pass. As she sat in the car facing downhill petrified with fear, the temptation to turn around grew to be overwhelming. Nevertheless, she shook off her fears, gripped the steering wheel, put the car in drive and pressed on to complete her trip. Still, the separation from her family continued to be painful, drawing her to tears every morning.

"I would just dust myself off and get to work," remembers Victoria who went on to successfully complete that project and accept other challenges along the way that ranged from partner horror stories to divorce to near bankruptcy.

"I am resolved to pay attention and learn from my foibles," said Victoria.

Mentors had a great influence on the development of Victoria's business. The single most important mentor was her first partner and good friend, Mary. Even though Mary was younger than Victoria, her positive and adventurous outlook on life was an inspiration.

"She trusted the goodness in people and taught me to always look for the positive in people and situations," said Victoria. "Together, we felt we could take on the world, and I believe the parts of the world we touched enjoyed our enthusiasm."

More often than not Victoria's other mentors were other small business owners who were her clients. In working to help them market their business, she was able to learn about their businesses, their dreams, their disappointments and their understanding of what it takes to be successfully self-employed. She had a banker who believed in her early on and extended a loan to her that would probably be difficult to obtain in today's market. She put her in the company of competent professionals—a good accountant and retired businessmen who not only encouraged her and rooted for her, but also provided sage advice.

"It's not like I had one confidant or primary mentor, but many who offered insight and advice," she said. "There is abundant opportunity to learn and grow in business surrounding everyone, usually, if you're just curious and ask questions, most people love to share and offer advice."

Conferences, seminars and organizations such as the Small Business Administration and the Chamber of Commerce became a strong part of Victoria's weekly activities, because they offered networking opportunities where she could learn new things. It was through these discovery experiences that she developed a relationship with other mentors to guide her.

"Whatever challenge you are facing, someone has been there before and knows the way," said Victoria. "Don't isolate yourself—ever. Become and stay active in your community."

Victoria's business was starting to grow but not without trials.

"For years, the business was undercapitalized and I chewed my fingernails wondering if I was going to make payroll or the rent," she said. "There were many things that kept me going, not the least of which were the wonderful people and vendors that continually pulled for us and who were willing to work with me.... And we had fun along the way—which is probably the most important ingredient to our success."

Today, at fifty-two, Victoria has grown her business, Discovery Map International, to twenty-one franchises from Amelia Island, Florida, to West Yellowstone, Montana, and several employees including her son. In 2008, the company's sales were $1.7 million. Not bad for a woman whose business started inside no more than a closet in a cabin in a small Idaho town.

A challenged economy has been hard on the travel industry, reaching Victoria's business and franchisees as well. She has had to learn to reevaluate her goals, resulting in employee layoffs, reduced spending and a reduction in her own compensation among other challenges.

"All businesses have risk," said Victoria. "You can't lose sight of the dream. You have to keep going when the going gets tough."

Victoria's future goals include mentoring others as she attributes her success to mentors who beat the odds and inspired her to think outside of the box. One such mentor was her grandmother—a strong-willed, self-made and eccentric woman.

"All my business experience has been learned through the School of Hard Knocks," said Victoria, whose formal education extends only through high school graduation. "The challenges I faced have forced me to learn, grow, risk, adapt and have a sense of humor."

Remember: Find mentors along the way who are willing and able to make time for you. Be like a sponge and learn! Who do you think might advise you?

Exercise #2
From Rule No. 2: Find a Mentor in an Offbeat Place

The Mentor/Mentee Quiz

Directions: Answer the following questions about the mentor-mentee relationships and the mentoring process.

1. Who drives and owns the mentoring partnership?

2. What seems to be the minimum mentor-mentee contact time that makes a positive difference in the mentee?

3. What two key things does a formal mentor do?

4. What is the mentoring skill that mentees value and remember most?

5. How many times should you give positive reinforcement for every correction or criticism you give? (For mentors)

6. What are five skills of a good mentor?

7. What are some things to do to get acquainted and build the mentor/mentee relationship?

8. What are three things that mentoring sessions are not?

9. What's one way to fail as a mentor? (Mentors only)

10. What's one way to fail as a mentee? (Mentees only)

Answers:
1. The mentee (but the mentor should help him/her successfully do this).
2. 1-2 hours per month.
3. Helps mentee identify goal(s) and build skills to reach the goal(s).
4. Encouragement.
5. At least four.
6. Listens actively; identifies goals, clarifies reality; builds trust; encourages.
7. Share your career history; share information about families; find common interests either in life experience, sports, hobbies, children, etc.; ask questions; tell why you're interested in the relationship, talk about past mentoring experiences.
8. Counseling, psychotherapy, gripe sessions.
9. Say, "Call me if you need me." (Not schedule specific contact time.)
10. Not to deliver on what was discussed at the last mentoring session. To not drive the relationship.

Chapter Three

Rule No. 3

Surround Yourself with People Whose Strengths Are Your Weaknesses and Give Away the Glory

In my role as the executive director of Ohio Valley General Hospital Foundation, the president of the hospital taught me two important rules for work:

1. Surround yourself with people who possess your weaknesses as their strengths.
2. Give away the glory.

Regarding the first rule, take a lesson from the politicians of the world. They wisely have entourages of people who help them fill in the gaps for everything that is not their areas of expertise. They have speechwriters, analysts, strategists, economists, defense experts and more waiting in the wings every day to offer advice. These people are usually not their relatives or best friends.

Human nature calls us to surround ourselves with people like us. That's great if you are talking about the person with whom you'll watch the football game or sit at the pool. We are comfortable around people like ourselves. But if you are talking about making changes that will bring about a greater good for you and those around you, you need to define your weaknesses and then surround yourself with people who fill in those gaps. They may not be the people you call when you want a sympathetic ear. But my guess is that you will need a sympathetic ear less often if you are successful in what you do, thus leaving more time to be with true friends.

Think about it: If you are wonderfully creative and a risk taker you are probably ahead in the innovative aspects of your work and life, but you may not have clear processes and accountability in line when you are being innovative. Probably you let things slip through the cracks, because you forget about the details or aren't even aware that they needed attention. Surround yourself with people who can help you strike a good balance between innovation and structure. Oftentimes in a marriage one spouse will be creative and less structured and this person will find a spouse who is more left brain strong and organized. A good balance is a bonus.

Perhaps you may be very organized and methodical and are the person who provides the information needed to make clear and concise decisions. But the path in which those decisions lead may not be clear to you. The pitfalls and risks may seem too great to move forward. If that is the case, surround yourself with the creative energy needed to articulate the effects of different scenarios.

Let's assume that you have the right people around you and are poised to succeed. Goals need to be defined in order to meet that success. You can't get somewhere if you don't know where you are going. Chances are that the main goal you want to achieve is going to remain your goal unless you can involve the team in setting and defining the parameters of the goal. If you engage a team in the goal setting process, they will want to be a part of the success and work harder toward it. Let them own the rewards of the team's success.

Once you reach your team's goal, do you feel as if you have done a great job? No. The team did a great job. You simply were the leader.

Just because you lead a team does not mean that you solely own the team's success. The team owns the success. As a matter of fact, I suggest that you give away the glory of the success solely to the team. "I want to thank all of you for the work that you did to make this possible. Your outstanding dedication to the mission at hand is what made this happen."

Being able to motivate people is one of the best skills you can have. It will multiply your effectiveness. Motivation will engage people to buy. It will engage people to follow you. It will engage people to trust you. It will engage people to help you. The single best way to motivate people that I know of is to continue to reinforce their positive contributions by applauding them personally, thus validating their efforts. Giving them the glory is an excellent way to do this.

As the former president of a company at which I was employed once told me, "What do you care if others get the credit? You are measured by what it is you can accomplish. If you can motivate others to help you get there, you don't need the credit. The results are what matters."

Surround yourself with people who not only have your weaknesses as their strengths; surround yourself with people from whom you can learn to be a better leader.

Rule Break: Employers give personality profile tests to prospective hires in order to tell their strengths and weaknesses. Interviewees are used to these tests and know what an employer is looking to see. If you truly want to get to know someone in any situation, ask the person open-ended questions that are behavioral in nature and will give you insight into how they respond to unanticipated situations. Sample questions may include:

* "What was the biggest disappointment in your life—both personal and professional—and how did you deal with it?"
* "What was the most gratifying thing that ever happened to you?"
* "What is the culture of your corporation?"
* "What was the best compliment you ever received?"
* "What was the worst criticism?"

How to Fill in Your Weakness Gaps:
1. Write down all of your personal and professional strengths.
2. Write down all of your personal and professional weaknesses. Please be honest.
3. If you are hiring people or looking for a group with which to become affiliated for professional or social reasons, choose people whose strengths are your weaknesses.
4. If you are seeking new friends, choose a mixture of both.

How to Give Away the Glory:
1. Tape a small sticky note with "Give Away the Glory" written on it to the bottom margin of your computer monitor as a reminder.
2. Get a small notebook or start a document on your computer and label it "Good Glories", where you can write down every time you have complimented someone on his or her work. Get in the habit of looking at it to remind yourself of how often you compliment others.

3. Next time you work with someone on a project, whether it be your place of worship, your children's school, your local library or at work, make note of every time you compliment someone on the job he or she is doing.
4. Be specific on how you praise the person's "glory." A simple "thank you" only shows that you are grateful. "You went above and beyond expectations when you stayed until 7:00 last evening to make sure that everything was prepared for today's presentation. Because of your work the presentation could not have been more effective. Thank you for your expertise and dedication."
5. Send a note stating your appreciation and the person's specific example of "glory" to his or her home. Those notes often find themselves saved for eternity.
6. Place a reminder in your calendar to analyze this list once a week at first and then once a month. You will see the list grow if you follow this process.

Remember: It is important to find out what your strengths and weaknesses are early on, so you can improve upon your presentation when looking for a job.

Exercise #3
From Rule No. 3: Surround Yourself with People Whose Strengths Are Your Weaknesses and Give Away the Glory

Fill in Your Weakness Gaps

Personal Strengths	Professional Strengths	Personal Weaknesses (WEAKNESS GAP)	Professional Weaknesses (WEAKNESS GAP)

Give the Glory Away Chart

Date	Name of Glory Beneficiary	His/Her Act of Glory	How I Recognized It

Are there lots of entries?

What is your goal per week?

Chapter Four

Rule No. 4

Your Favorite Place is Not the Coffee Shop or the Couch; Now it is the Bookstore

I love to stop at my favorite coffee shop not only to have a wonderfully rich and overpriced cup of coffee but also to experience the friendly atmosphere of seeing others overspend for the same experience. Television is a wonderfully passive way to enjoy a relaxing evening and live vicariously through experiences that I would never enter into awake. However, neither a cappuccino nor my couch helps me get to where I ultimately want to be. They are fine ways to treat myself to an escape or an hour with a friend—things we all need. Alternatively, a bookstore is filled with books that challenge your way of thinking, teach you about the things you do not know and opens the doors to reach new uncharted roads.

Libraries are also a wonderful place to find reference books for your new journey. Some libraries do not have the extensive list of current nonfiction books that a bookstore may have. Yet most city libraries have reciprocal agreements with other libraries and can get a particular book upon request. Compare and draw your own conclusion. There may be a book you cannot afford to buy on your present budget. Request it from your local library.

Not sure what you want to do? Go to the business section of your local bookstore and you will find shelves full of ideas. Not sure how you will handle a particular transition in your life such as divorce or loss of a job? Go to the self-help section of the bookstore and you will find countless options. Want to learn how to start a business, sell real estate, train your dog or sell something online? The bookstore!

At some large bookstores, you will be able to get your cup of coffee, sit in the café and read books there. You think this may frustrate the bookseller, but I bet she'll be happy you're there. You will purchase many books during your round of *Chutes and Ladders*.

The Internet is another wonderful resource of information as well, but there is a lot more useless information to weed through on the Internet than there is in a bookstore. It costs a lot of money for publishing companies to produce books. It does not cost a lot of money to get a Web site up and running. For information to actually make it to the published stage that hits a bookstore, it has to be editorially scrutinized followed by a market analysis on the viability of the book and the creation of a marketing plan. All of these require substantial financial investment. Editorial departments of publishing companies do some of the work for you when it comes to researching credible information.

Where I find the Internet most helpful is in gathering resources not readily available in the bookstores, such as interactive venues that can give you valuable feedback on your specific situation. Examples of these would be personality profile tests or salary estimators that appear on career management sites such as www.monster.com or www.usajobs.com, where you can access a list of government jobs which are not mentioned in the newspaper.

There are wonderful nonfiction books that will help you learn what you need to know, and there are just as many that should have been reduced to magazine articles. Make sure that the books you invest in will give you specific strategies to help you on your journey. Spending some time in the café looking them over will help you determine which books will ultimately be good choices.

During the time I was changing my life plan, I remember thinking that I had a lot of energy to put into something that was going to turn my life around. I knew that I was dedicated to doing whatever it took to work it. The problem was that I didn't know what that "something" should be. So I spent hours sitting on the floor and in the cafés of book stores leafing through various books on entrepreneurial ideas, starting a business, sales and promotions.

I just could not find the direction I needed to follow. I was listening but could not hear the calling. I decided this was okay, I'd be patient. I just kept reading, taking classes in basic computer skills and talking to people who were in jobs that seemed interesting to me.

In reading, I was able to channel some of that unguided energy I had into learning things I didn't know in an area of interest to me. Now you might think you need to be scholarly to be a reader, which couldn't be farther from the truth. Good current nonfiction is written for the adult learner; not like a textbook that a student in college or a researcher might read but more like a conversation that holds anecdotal stories and points that are engaging and centered on a theme. I was never a compliant reader when it came to textbooks—I think I was an adult learner far before I was an adult.

I love to write, so I became a student of becoming a better writer. I read books on creative writing and the art and style of good writing. I read books by bestselling authors. I read books by my author friends. I read books once for the experience and reread them again to study the craft of how they were written.

This helped me acquire more work when I was a freelance writer for the *Pittsburgh Post-Gazette* as well as other publications.

Publicity and marketing interested me as well, because I could see how language in different contexts could carry very different messages. The art of strong language is very powerful and the lack of skill in language could lead to weak or nonexistent persuasion.

Soon I began reading about sales, self-promotion and business during this period of my life when I had time on my hands but was not sure of my direction. I call this "meanwhile" time. During this time, I had a lot of energy and just didn't know what to do with it. I honed my skills by reading and trying new things. This is when I mentored under an advertising specialty executive where I put to good work my newly acquired knowledge of sales and studied what motivated people to buy.

I went on to study management and then on to earn a professional certification in association management. While you have time and are not tied down to a full-time job, read everything you can, take courses in computer and other skills that you don't have or in which you need more expertise and study for certifications that will help you later. Once you get going in your new career, you won't have time to do these things. Do it in your "meanwhile" time.

Again, if you are not sure what kind of work you want to pursue or what kind of business you want to open, read. Reading is a good way to channel energy and open new doors.

Rule Break: Don't always purchase books by the bestselling authors or ones with flashy covers. If you want to change careers, ask the bookseller for recommendations; if you want to start a business, ask the bookseller for a good book by a successful entrepreneur. Maybe the person lives locally and could be your mentor. If you are good with people, read through the titles on sales techniques. Chances are if people like you and are willing to buy whatever product you're selling, a sales career might be in your future. If you are not sure what direction you want to take, read through the titles in the business or self-help sections.

Five Rules for Picking a Nonfiction Book That Will Stay in Your Library Forever:
1. *Open the book and look at the pages.* If you see a lot of copy with few breaks or little white space on the page, you will know that the book will read more like a novel. If you see a lot of white space, lots of breaks in format and many bold headlines, you will know that the specific points may be more easily accessible when you are trying to reference them at a later date. This format may prove to be more accessible for readers looking for a "how-to..."
2. *Look for lists.* Lists will give you specific instructions of what to do and not to do to jumpstart your journey. Lists are simple and practical.
3. *Read the table of contents.* If the table of contents doesn't answer the question of what the chapter is about, chances are the book will be just as hard in which to find relevant points you need. Ask yourself, "Will the contents of these chapters specifically answer the questions I have?"
4. *Read the inside back cover to see what the author has accomplished his or herself.* The author should have been there and done that.
5. *If you purchase a book, go home and read a chapter only to realize you have made a mistake, take it back.* We return clothes, jewelry, food and more. Return the book and choose another. Booksellers want you to be a regular and happy customer.

Ruth's Story
Through most of Ruth Kuttler's life, she felt stuck in a place called *mediocrity* where she was unhappy and unfulfilled. She felt that "settling" was her lot in life and accepted it. She grew up with the fairy tale concept that a woman's career didn't matter since her real job was to manage her family. Career was meant to be something a woman fell back on just in case she had to work.

"At that time there were two careers for women," said Ruth. "Nurse or teacher." Her mother wanted her to become a nurse and so she did, graduating with high honors, marrying, earning a master's degree in nursing and going on to become a physician's assistant. Still, nursing did not seem to be her calling. Western medicine seemed out of alignment with her philosophy of more natural forms of healing.

After twenty-five years in healthcare, Ruth received what she now says was a gift—she was laid off. At the time, depression set in quickly and she began to self-examine what she was truly called to do with her life. One morning while reading the newspaper she spotted a poetry contest. She wasn't a poet and didn't even like poetry, but for some reason she kept going back to that contest thinking that if she wrote about how she was feeling, she could figure out the rest of her life. Ruth sat down to write the poem "Going Not Where I Know" and didn't put her pen down for three weeks. There were days she wrote for twelve hours straight without getting dressed, making meals or doing anything else.

Along with the words of her poems came new ideas that transformed her beliefs about herself and possibilities of creating the life she wanted to live.

"Through my poetry I came to understand that God was talking to me and directing me to follow my heart," said Ruth. "For the first time I felt empowered to do whatever it took to design the life I really wanted."

Ruth vowed then to let go of self-limiting beliefs and fears. She distanced herself from non-supportive people and started to read personal development books and attend seminars of the like. She participated in empowering activities such as Toastmasters. She stayed away from the news as well as friends and family who were negative about her pursuits and instead spent her free time reading positive books such as Napoleon Hill's classic *Think and Grow Rich* and Stephen Covey's *The 7 Habits of Highly Effective People*.

"I closed the chapter on a twenty-five-year career to start my life over again," said Ruth, who realized she could not make a living writing poetry but had confidence that she could put her writing and creative talents to good use.

"Little by little I started to replace the beliefs that controlled my whole life," said Ruth.

She saw the Internet as her future and, at forty-six, enrolled in classes to build her computer skills, living on credit cards and a home equity line of credit. She took courses in software programs such as Dreamweaver, Photoshop, Illustrator and more. She ultimately decided to start a business designing Web sites and helping people with Internet marketing.

Today, eleven years later, Ruth is the owner of a successful business specializing in Web design, business development and marketing called WebPuzzleMaster.com, which she operates from her home where she and her husband live in Naples, Florida.

"I truly believe there are no accidents," said Ruth. "Whatever we believe and think about we attract into our lives. I make a point of visualizing what I want every day."

Ruth began her business with a partner and is now solo. She has no employees and outsources all work she does not do from her home office. Her niche is her ability to harmonize a personal touch and good writing into all aspects of Web design and marketing.

Her only regret is that she did not have a mentor along the way. "I could have learned these lessons earlier in life," she said. Because of this, Ruth's goal is to continue to mentor the many people who come to her for advice. "Be persistent," she tells them. "You can't throw in the towel, because the first thing you do does not work."

She advises others to not allow themselves to stay in a stifling environment. "Don't be complacent to sit back and do a menial job in the easiest way possible," she said. "Make it into the best opportunity it can be. If you see something that can be better, do whatever you can to make it better."

What books have you read that reinforce this philosophy? Would a trip to the bookstore or library help you discover a new one?

Remember: Have you made arrangements to find a mentor? If not, do it now.

Exercise #4
From Rule No. 4: Your Favorite Place is Not the Coffee Shop or the Couch; Now it is the Bookstore

Non-Fiction Book Categories for
When You Are Not Sure of Your Calling

If you are not sure where to begin your quest for a new journey, spend time looking over some of these sections of traditional non-fiction categories in your local bookstore. Ask the bookseller to help you locate titles that marry these sections with your personal interests.

1. Self-Help
2. Business Management
3. Sales
4. Inspirational
5. Biographies
6. Media Relations
7. Public Speaking
8. Entrepreneurs
9. Starting a Business
10. Self-Promotion

Internet Resources to Help You Find Your Way

Salary estimates for specific professions in specific cities: www.salary.com

O*Net—Occupational Information Network: Interests Profiler and more—the nation's primary source on career information: www.onetcenter.org

U.S. Department of Labor's site for job seekers: www.careeronestop.org

Organize your job search—Post a question, etc.: www.cvtips.com

Apprenticeship Training Resources: www.khake.com/page58.html

Occupational Outlook Handbook by the Bureau of Labor Statistics: www.bls.gov/OCO

Federal/State/Local Government jobs: www.USAjobs.com

Templates for business plans, competitive analysis, start-up cost estimates and more: www.score.org/business_toolbox.html

Career Cruising—interactive way to explore different career options: www.careercruising.com

Small Business Administration small business planner: www.sba.gov/smallbusinessplanner/index.html

Starting over after divorce: www.womansdivorce.com/inspiration.html

Where freelancers bid on posted projects (web design, writing, etc.): www.elance.com or www.gofreelance.com

Starting Over for Women: www.makingbreadmagazine.com

Chapter Five

Rule No. 5

Make Your "Wheel of Fortune" Spin on Balance

If your career is consuming too much of your life, you will not be able to succeed at the rate you want. You will burn yourself out before you get to where you want to be. Here is how you will know whether or not you are heading down this *chute*. You feel tired, irritable and overwhelmed. You notice you haven't seen close friends in a while. The people who are close to you are asking for more of your time and you feel as if you just don't have any more time to give. You find that you are not doing the things that you used to enjoy—walking, meeting friends for coffee or visiting your favorite shop perhaps. You are working on your computer until you go to bed. You are not sleeping well.

Conversely, if you are not focusing enough time on re-charting your life you may find that you are not moving forward and susceptible to feeling victimized. Going through a life transition such as losing a job, getting a divorce or seeking new employment can be both challenging and devastating. It is almost as if you are going through the stages of grief. Allow yourself the time to mourn the losses of your past, but keep from feeling like a victim. Be proactive. Identify what it is that you miss. Really examine the basis of what you miss and what you want in the future. Do you miss the old job or do you miss the financial and emotional security of a steady paycheck? Do you miss a person or do you miss the dream of happily ever after? Are there not other ways to establish financial security? Are there dream police who say you cannot create a new dream?

What is it about your situation that you can change in order to bring you more peace and happiness? You probably cannot get your old job back. You may not even want to. But you can use the extra time you have to truly define what it is that you do want. Envision it as if there are no barriers. Once you know what you want, you can chart a course to get there. This is where you begin to take action. You will no longer feel victimized. Make sure that what you want is something you can feel—not see. The only thing you should see is *yourself* in your "Success Sketch" enjoying your new life!

A healthy life is one in which all areas are in balance: relationships/ home, spiritual/community, social/cultural, financial/career, personal development/educational and health/appearance. Do a self-evaluation of your life in each of these categories. Are you spending time nurturing each of these areas for yourself? Are you celebrating the holidays by getting out your decorations? Are you spending time meditating, reflecting, worshiping or praying? Have you seen a play or attended a library lecture on a topic that interests you? Are you meeting with a mentor? When is the last time you met a friend for coffee? Have you signed up for a yoga class or a class on Microsoft Office? Are you eating heart-healthy foods? Have you taken those close to you or just yourself on a vacation that could be as simple as an overnight at a friend's or family member's house?

Change requires a dream—a goal. Envision yourself feeling what you want to feel and every day you will feel it coming closer and closer to you. Don't let negative self-talk get you off track. "Self-talk" can be a deterrent when you are in the middle of a challenge, because it can tend to be negative, a distraction and can spiral out of control if fear is involved.

Have you ever worked hard toward something, wanted it more than anything, put everything you have into achieving it, only to find yourself worrying that it won't happen and then imagining the disasters that will follow as a result?

After my husband and I separated, I worked very hard at trying to get through the litigious process of divorce. Previously I had cosigned loans for his business, a place I did not work or make decisions, against my better judgment. Note to self—trust your judgment and do your best not to go against it just to keep peace. Start creating alternatives that are in line with your good judgment.

I had worked hard to prepare for the hearing, organized everything for my attorney that I could, practiced what I was to say and talked to as many people as I could about the upcoming hearing to save my house from creditors to the business. But negative self-talk began to get in the way. "I am going to lose." "The children and I are going to be thrown out on the street without a place to live." "I am never going to be able to take care of the children." "How am I going to handle all of this?" It wasn't at all productive and did nothing but deter me from peace, balance and moving forward. It just instilled fear.

Well, I lost the hearing. Our very nice home in an exclusive suburb whose mortgage was nearly paid off did indeed go toward paying off my ex-husband's business debt. The children and I became homeless, carless, without health insurance and hungry. Was this fair? Of course not. But what guarantees that life is fair? It's not about what is fair. It's about what you do with the cards you've been dealt.

Look at celebrities who have a multitude of power, fame, money and attention. Look at how many end up seeking the comfort of vices. What are they seeking comfort from? Look at how many have been through countless bouts in rehabilitation facilities. Don't they have everything anyone could ever want? Or do they? Do they know who truly likes them for who they are inside instead of the status of who they have become? Do people flock to them because of their fame and money or because they are good people? If you are soundly grounded in who you are and value the intangibles such as love, relationships and integrity, then power, fame and "stuff" can be part of your life, not define who you are.

Additionally, if you value "stuff", you will never have enough of it. There is always more to have. The appetite is insatiable. So when are you satisfied? Never. It is a pretty dooming philosophy and the very reason rehabilitation programs try to teach people new values and a new direction of a life dedicated to service to others and surrendering to a higher calling (both intangibles).

I look back now and can clearly see that worrying about what might occur did absolutely nothing to help me fix it. And in spite of all that happened, the world did not come to an end.

One night I lay in bed looking up at the ceiling and said to myself, "I still have a roof over my head. We had dinner tonight. I have food for the children tomorrow. I have people close to me who care about us."

My negative self-talk was wasted energy. Not only did it do nothing to help me, but it wasn't even reasonable. I began to realize I could handle the situation and indeed was able to take care of and support my children.

Eventually, I set myself on a career path whereby I was able to purchase a car and another house in the same school district. It was the tools I am conveying that helped me to get there.

What I truly feared was that I could not control what was going on around me and the unknown was scary. I had not been able to make my marriage work. I did not control the household income and I did not control the court system.

I had worked so hard at doing the best I could at what I was able to control—improving my skills as a writer, taking on new clients, supporting my children—that I built a delusion: If I worked hard enough, I could control anything. What a comedy that was. Finally, I woke up from my own nightmare and the garden of virtues I had been blessed with began to bloom around me.

Most of what was going on in the courts was out of my hands. So finally I asked myself, "Why fear it?" Chances are that the worst-case scenario in any situation, with the exception of health, is still something that can be overcome. I was blessed with good health. I began celebrating the good things in my life.

Practice positive messages for your self-talk such as "I can do this." Imagine how you will feel when you actually accomplish your goal. Remember that feeling. Imagine how it will feel over and over in your mind.

A good friend suggested that I write "God is synchronizing" on a piece of paper and post the adage where I could see it every day. I wrote the words on a neon pink index card and hung them above my stove. I took that card with me when I moved to my new house and posted it in my new kitchen. My old friends weren't there to help me through that move, but my new friends were. A new life was unfolding in front of me. I was like a child in a candy shop and I couldn't have been more excited to be there. I was discarding old thoughts, superficial friendships and insignificant activities like yesterday's newspaper. I was relishing new quality friendships, new interests and the new home I was creating for my family.

Life holds a wonderful opportunity to harmonize love, work, service, education and friendships for a greater good. Work on these intangible values to evolve and grow. Balance your life to appreciate every aspect of what the world is offering you.

Take time to reward yourself. This new quest in life will test you often. You have and will be met with rejection. Be sure to celebrate the small successes. If a potential employer calls you for an interview, reward yourself with a cup of your favorite tea. Make time to reward the important people in your life for their small successes as well.

Rule Break: We have been told since we were children that if we put others first, we will be happy. I believe and have seen this to be true. Doing things for others not only nurtures your own soul, but the bonds created with the people receiving your kindness often strengthen your personal relationships with them as well, again nurturing your soul even more. I say now is a time to broaden your interpretation of the Golden Rule—"Do unto others as you would have them do unto you." I say, "Do also for yourself as you do unto others." When things are really challenging, it is hard to make time to help others. Additionally, it can be even harder to prioritize doing special things for yourself. Remember that you are taking on a big life transition. Plants don't grow without sun and nourishment. Lives don't either. Be sure to nurture yourself along with the others in your life.

Eight Steps to Keep Your Life in Balance for Better Success:
1. *Do a life balance self-examination.* List these aspects of a balanced life and next to each element put a percentage of the time and energy you spend on them: relationships/home, spiritual/community, social/cultural, financial/career, personal development/educational and health/appearance. These should total 100 percent. Draw a circle and divide it into a pie chart representing the corresponding percentages. Mark your calendar six months from now to complete this pie chart again and compare. Is it more in balance?
2. *Write each of the six life balance areas on the top of one index card (six cards total) and list at least one specific goal under each area with a deadline for achieving it.* Remember, "I will find more time for social outings" is not a goal. "I will organize a women's night out once a month with three friends and have the first one by mid-February" is a specific goal with a deadline. As you achieve one goal, check it off and write down the next one. You may have more than one goal at a time in a specific area. That is more than okay! Look at your goals every day. Mark your calendar in six months to update your goals.
3. *Have someone over for a simple lunch or dinner at least once a month.* Connecting with friends and family is important during any life transition. These friends and family will keep you from becoming isolated.

Isolation will keep you from creating new dreams and taking action to bring your dreams to reality. Entertaining also requires some creative thought. Create a menu with new recipes. It will help you stretch out of your comfort zone.

4. *Go to a meditative or spiritual location once a week to give thanks for what you have.* Sitting quietly in a park, church, temple, mosque or sunlit corner once a week will give you the right venue in which to reflect on your progress over the last week. Song and prayer will help you give thanks for what you have. Listen to the silence. It is there that you will find answers.

5. *Use an inexpensive bookkeeping software program or a ledger to keep track of your finances.* It is much easier to feel at ease with your financial situation when you know exactly what it is. Set up a standard account and track your expenses. Keep a separate category for "business" expenses. Your expenses that are related to finding a job or going into your own business may be able to be deducted—even before you find a job or start a new business. Check with your accountant. Analyze your spending on a monthly basis. Are there areas in which you can spend less? Can your savings afford you a trip to the movies or a concert?

6. *Take a class or see a counselor for a fresh perspective.* When you are trying to change things in your life, old non-productive habits can get in the way. A counselor can help you identify these old habits so that you can begin to change them. If you do not feel a counselor is necessary or cannot afford one, sign up for a class in something that will get you closer to your "Success Sketch." Keeping your mental capacity fresh and stimulated will propel you up *ladders* and keep you from the *chutes*.

7. *Join a professional or social organization on a topic that interests you.* This could be a book club, church, synagogue, meditative meeting place or an association for your profession. Make sure it is a place where you will meet new people. The social aspect of this will be as rewarding as what you will learn. To find social and cultural clubs, locate your city's cultural newspaper. For business organizations, read your local business or metropolitan newspaper.

8. *Start walking on a regular basis.* Regular exercise will give you more energy and keep your mind alert. Any form of exercise will suffice—yoga, Pilates, a visit to the gym. Walking is simple and anyone can do it. Consult with your doctor before commencing any rigorous exercise routine.

Judy's Story

As a young woman with four sons, Judy Briggs found herself divorced and not able to make ends meet on one salary. In order to improve her chances of finding a good job to support her eight-year-old twins as well as her one-year-old and four-year-old, she went back to school and earned a bachelor's degree in Business Administration. The process led her to mentor her boys in the value of an education. They all studied together as a family at the table every night.

After earning her degree, she and her sons moved to another town for a good job opportunity, only to find that she still was not earning enough to support her family. There were weeks when she had only twenty dollars in her wallet for gas, groceries and children's lunch money. She took on a second job as a waitress.

"I kept thinking, 'There has got to be more to life than this,'" remembers Judy, who had realized also that her demanding work schedules were now causing her to miss her sons' activities.

"When you work you can't go to baseball games," remembers Judy in regards to watching her children grow up around her while not participating in the experience as much as she had wanted. "I was missing great years."

While Judy was juggling kids, activities, jobs and finances she began to realize that there was one thing she could no longer juggle and that was the plethora of "stuff" that had accumulated around her house. The experience of moving to a new city and all of the boys' sports activities led to a collection of furniture and gear that she no longer had room to store. However, she couldn't find anybody to haul it away. That's when she became familiar with and eventually bought a franchise in 1-800-Got-Junk? It was then that she realized work could be fun.

The young and energetic culture of the company is what drew Judy to it. 1-800-Got-Junk? is a professional junk removal company that provides space and time for clients. They take over the chore and time invested in hauling things away, 90 percent of which is recycled for further use.

"It's not a normal company—in a good way," said Judy. "They encourage crazy ideas."

On regular occasions Judy and her crew, which, at times, has included all of her sons, will park the truck near an intersection in their town of Framingham, Massachusetts, and stand on the roof in blue wigs and start dancing to entertain the crowd.

"People laugh and have fun with us," said Judy, who stresses that her team continually asks customers why they chose her company and how her team can make their experience better.

Judy embraced the culture of the company and capitalized on it with her franchise. Her business degree came in handy as she set a goal plan for the business, which has up to twenty-two employees in the warmer months.

"Never did I think that employees would show up a half-hour early for work and leave a half-hour late," said Judy who provides a pool table, fitness equipment and a dartboard for her employees. "I have to tell them, 'Come on guys, I want to go home.'"

Judy endured challenges along the way that included another divorce as well as debt. She went back to school to earn her MBA, which she feels has accelerated her success. In 2008 her revenue was $1.25 million. She belongs to the Entrepreneurs' Organization and has mentored many people including her children, whom she says push themselves because of how they witnessed her do the same. Her oldest twin recently returned from Iraq to the rigor of college, where he told his mother that he never realized how much he had learned about business working for her.

"And they thought it was all about hauling junk," laughs Judy. "I provided them with more than just a paycheck."

Judy was early to recognize the value of balancing time with her children, the ability to make her own schedule even if it involved eighty-hour weeks at first and being able to develop good relationships with her family members, her employees and the business community. She attributes her success to her ability to focus and stay positive as well as her "failure is not an option" mind-set and her great team and family.

Find the balance in your life. Are you noticing that the things you value are not the things you spend most of your time doing? If so, what is your plan to change that?

Remember: Place your Success Sketch where you can see it each and every day.

Exercise #5
From Rule No. 5: Make Your "Wheel of Fortune" Spin on Balance

The Life Balance Chart and Goals

1. The Life Balance Self-Examination: Next to the areas of a balanced life listed below put a percentage of the time and energy you spend on each: relationships/home, spiritual/community, social/cultural, financial/career, personal development/educational and health/appearance. These should total 100 percent. Draw a circle and divide it into a pie chart representing the corresponding percentages. Mark your calendar six months from now to complete this pie chart again and compare. Is it in balance?

_____ % Relationships/Home

_____ % Spiritual/Community

_____ % Social/Cultural

_____ % Financial/Career

_____ % Personal Development/
          Educational

_____ % Health/Appearance

100%   TOTAL

2. The Life Balance Goal Cards: Write each of the six areas above on the top of one index card (six cards total). Write them on a piece of paper if you do not have index cards. List at least one specific goal under each area with a deadline for achieving it. Remember, "I will find more time for social outings" is not a goal. "I will organize a women's night out once a month with three friends and have the first one by mid February" is a specific goal with a deadline. More than one goal per card is okay! Are they SMART Goals? (Specific, Measurable, Attainable, Results Oriented and Time Framed.)

	Relationship/ Home	Spiritual/ Communi.	Social/ Cultural	Financial/ Career	Pers. Dev./Ed.	Health/ Appear.
Goal #1						
Goal #2						

Chapter Six

Rule No. 6

Offer Solutions to Problems– Name the Company's Pain

When was the last time you read in the newspaper that a Fortune 500 company had a number of employees with outstanding degrees and skills on their résumés? Probably never. When was the last time you read that a Fortune 500 company had exceeded its sales from the previous year, merged with another company to offer better services or was expanding to better meet the needs of its customers? Probably more often.

Often job seekers and entrepreneurs concentrate on the skills they have when they are seeking work or customers. Instead, concentrate on the benefits you offer instead of the skills you have. You are not a person who can answer the phone or keep a spreadsheet; you have managed an office so that the professionals can focus on their patients or customers without distractions. You are not only able to use Word, Quark, InDesign and PhotoShop; you have a track record of providing all the communication services necessary for a business to increase sales.

Companies and their human resources departments as well as customers do not as much care about your skills as they care about how you can make their lives easier, more productive and profitable. That means you have to have proven results. Intent and flowery language in résumés tells them what you can do is irrelevant. The only thing that matters is what you have accomplished. Your proven track record takes the risk out of hiring you.

Work is not the only place where you may have solved problems. If you have managed a family budget, you have managed a business. If you have organized something in your church or children's school, you have met a need. If you have volunteered to help with a cause, you have helped others solve a problem.

The first way to show that you can solve a company's leading problem is to define it. If you are going into business for yourself, you need to ask yourself what need your product or service is meeting in society. If you can't answer that question, then start with something else. You must find a niche. If you are on an interview or trying to connect with someone at a networking event, be sure to ask the person what his or her biggest challenge is. He or she will be able to answer that question quickly and be happy to tell you, because it is the driving source of his or her unrest. It is what keeps one from achieving his or her goals and target profit margin and what keeps the person late at the office and away from the family. The challenge is what he or she fears the competition will be better able to do, thus eclipsing his or her business in the market, which may cost one a job and the ability to secure another job. It is what keeps people up at night.

Once you know where a company's pain is, make sure you communicate well how you can ease that pain. Additionally, and this is the most important part, demonstrate how you already have eased pain and been an effective problem solver for others. Show, don't tell.

When I sought the position of president of Forbes Health Foundation, I learned it was a large hospital foundation that had successfully raised money in the distant past for its work and hospice program, had not been successful in the last twenty-five years at fundraising for the hospital. Additionally, it had just endured a large economic setback—an affiliation with the largest hospital bankruptcy in United States history. Nevertheless, I was drawn to the challenge of the position and identified the thriving nature of the community as a potential area for success. Most of my friends and colleagues said I would be crazy to apply for a position so risky, which encouraged me more.

When I finally decided to throw my hat in the ring, unfortunately, the application period had already closed. "Fifty-eight people have applied for this position," I was told, "and we have some very qualified candidates already."

I decided to forgo pleading with the person in charge of the process to consider me and went directly to the president of the hospital. Why?

Because the position reported directly to him and he would be the one who would feel the pain if the person in this unfilled position did not solve the problem of raising money. The president, of course, was too busy to take my call so I quickly got to know his assistant (with whom I am still good friends today) and left a message that I was already succeeding at doing the job the president needed to have done at a similar hospital with similar challenges. I wanted to speak with him if only for the sake of giving some good advice.

The hospital president called me back—twice.

I told him that I knew the interview process was almost over, but if he gave me fifteen minutes of his time, I guaranteed that he would in the very least have a broader understanding of the challenges that lay ahead, which strategies will work and which will not.

His secretary called me the next morning with an interview time. I had two days to do research. I went on the hospital Web site and found out every relevant statistic I could about the hospital—what their leading service lines were, how many employees they had, where the hospital fell in relationship to the system of hospitals in which it belonged. I'd already researched the demographics of the community in which I would need to fundraise. I called everyone I knew who was strategically placed within the hospital and familiar with my work and asked them to make reference calls to the president on my behalf.

At the beginning of the interview, he focused on my past experience in overcoming challenges, some personal, and how tenacity, growth, faith, dedication and values led to my personal and professional success. This president had clearly done a lot of executive interviews and knew what to look for.

We talked about the challenges of the hospital; I asked him how he saw them.

I laced through our discussion advice on how I applied strategies in my current position to address those challenges with success. I was there for two hours. He asked me to return to be interviewed by the chairman of the board, who was the president of a successful company. I knew at that point I was being taken seriously as a candidate for the job.

Was I nervous? Sometimes I get nervous about other things, but I never get nervous about interviews, because I know that I can offer the person something his or her company needs. I realize my interviewer is probably nervous about hiring the wrong person, so it becomes my job to be the only applicant whom the interviewer can count on to get the job done. It takes confidence, not arrogance. Confidence and know-how. Be fearless, not reckless.

The chairman of the hospital board told me that they liked to hire people who have been through significant adversity, because they often end up being very hard and dedicated workers. I knew then that I wanted to work there. I wanted to be with an organization that valued tenacity, dedication and performance. They didn't care as much about what you said you could do as they cared about what you had already proven you could do. He went on to tell me that they were concerned that a fundraiser might be met with a lot of rejection, since the community had not experienced any fundraising for the hospital in twenty-five years and the hospital had just come off of a strong economic setback. I smiled and said, "Asking someone for money and having them say no is not the worst thing that has ever happened to me." He smiled. "Good answer," he said. "To a question I didn't even ask." Then he nodded and said, "People will like you here." I knew then that I had the job.

I built a fundraising program from the ground up at this hospital with a new board, new corporation, programs and staff. We had little to no donors when I started, but within a few years had broken our capital campaign goals twice to raise more than ten million dollars for a new emergency department, women's and infants' care centers and a heart and vascular center and one and a half million dollars for a new hospice.

The most rewarding part of this entire experience was not only being able to touch the lives of tens of thousands of patients served by these programs on an annual basis, but also being able to build a strong board of directors who are not only like family but also are mentors under whom I became a devoted apprentice. A good situation is where those around you trust and believe in you so much that they become your advocates as well as your friends. Develop relationships that make a meaningful difference in your life. Surround yourself with people you admire and learn from them. Partner with these people to solve important problems and celebrate your successes.

Rule Break: Listen and read what some experts tell you that you can't do. Examine all the reasons—you're too old, you're too young, you're too inexperienced, you're overqualified, you don't have enough financial backing, etc. Then, do it anyway. Because when you do, people will notice.

How to Be an Invaluable Problem Solver:
1. Get in the habit of asking people in your day-to-day life what their biggest challenges are. Then ask more questions that will help you create a solution.
2. Take your list of accomplishments and list next to each one the problem it solved. Be able to discuss how you got there.
3. Stay late regularly without being asked.
4. Show up early regularly without being asked.
5. Generate well developed ideas without being asked. Make sure those ideas solve problems.

Remember: Become a problem solver. Have you found somebody's pain? It might just help to ease your own.

Exercise #6
From Rule No. 6: Offer Solutions to Problems—
Name the Company's Pain

Problem Solving Checklist

It is helpful to solve problems with the input of others. Involve your whole team in this process. If you are on an interview, see if you can determine the root cause of the company's biggest challenge. Then offer how you can help with a solution. The following questions will help you determine the problem.

1. What is the problem?
2. Where is the problem happening?
3. When is it happening?
4. Who are the parties involved?
5. Did you draw the steps to what happened?
6. Were there alternatives that could have been considered?
7. Why is the problem happening? (Ask "Why?" again. Keep asking why five times until you have the root cause of the problem. Do a "Five Whys" for each alternative.)

Why?

Why?

Why?

Why?

Why?

8. What measures are being taken to solve the problem? By Whom? When?
9. How do we further prevent this from happening again?

Example:

Problem: The return percentage on our recent direct mail solicitation that was sent to a purchased mailing list of recipients is less than the national average. Why? Because we aren't sending it to the right people and/or we are using the wrong letter. Why? Because we thought we should purchase a mailing list and try a new audience and/or we used a letter from a staff member instead of a donor. Why? Because last year's letter did not do well either and we sent it to our existing donors and/or the letter we sent last year was from a staff member. Why? Because that's what we've always done.

Proposed Solution: Next time draft a letter from a donor and a letter from the president. Test market by sending the same number of letters to an existing donor audience and track which has a better return. Then, mail the rest of the letters from the author that had the most success and compare it to the return of the purchased list.

Chapter Seven

Rule No. 7

Your Résumé is Your Showcase of Results and Transferable Skills

Most résumé resources will tell you to keep your résumé simple, listing your skills, years of work experience and education. I suggest that you place your specific job and technical skills at the end of the résumé and precede them with a quantifiable list of accomplishments you achieved under each entity.

Keep in mind there is a high likelihood that a Generation Xer (born anywhere from 1965 to 1978) will be reviewing your résumé. If you are currently employed and seeking a new job, your work experience that is more than ten years old is irrelevant, because work has changed much since these dates and you will appear behind the times. Do not list the lifeguard job you had in high school. Highlight your latest and greatest accomplishments in terms that will appeal to youthful recruiters and hiring managers, customizing each résumé to directly address the needs of individual prospective employers. If you have not worked in years, list the last one or two jobs you had before you took the hiatus.

Include a "Key Accomplishments" section that will showcase your transferable skills. (See exercise 7 for a worksheet on defining "Transferable Skills.") List the accomplishments that were specific to the jobs under each specific job area of your résumé so that employers can see the pace of your professional growth.

"Key Accomplishments" are measurable ways in which you met obstacles and solved problems. What were some of the challenges you faced?

What actions did you take to overcome the problems? What were the results of your work? You didn't do two jobs when someone was laid off in your department—you produced twice the number of reports after the company downsized.

Think of your key accomplishments in the framework of transferable skills that can be applied to any career choice. Transferable skills fall into three categories: your abilities to *communicate, organize information* and *operate/fix equipment*. You may be good at instructing others or writing. You may be good at organizing data and keeping records. You may be good at fixing things and making things work. Demonstrate in your résumé your key accomplishments, keeping these transferable skills in mind.

When I was evaluating how I would support my family I could see that the allied health profession I left when I had my first child was not going to afford me the ability to support five people. Although I earned a decent salary, I assessed the things that I liked to do (write, communicate, be with people, motivate, lead), things that were important to me (due to my children, I could not travel out of town and I wanted to learn new things about leadership and management) and considered careers in which I could put those things to use to earn a better than average living. Sales seemed to fit the description. It seemed to me that aside from those who had vast histories of education behind them, those who could sell seemed able to move up the corporate ladder faster than those who were not in quantifiable professions. I sat down and defined what skills I already had that were transferable to a sales position. I could communicate well and enjoyed being with people. These were skills that transfered well to selling.

Rule Break: Remember that responsibilities are not achievements. You may have been responsible for bookkeeping, entering data or running events. But your achievements are that you created new strategies that enabled the organization to save thousands of dollars in expenses, created a database that allowed the company to process customer information twice as fast and created an event that raised tens of thousands.

How to Translate Your Volunteer Activities to Work Experience on Your Résumé:
1.   Make a list of every project that you have worked on beginning as far back as you can remember. These may include things like: Managed a Family Budget, Girl Scout Leader, Conference Organizer, Parent

Teacher Organization Treasurer. Just because you have not been receiving a salary does not mean you have not been working. If you have been at home for a number of years raising children or for other reasons, you most likely have been involved in productive but perhaps non-income earning work.

2. Next to each item on the list, write down all the things you accomplished while in that role. Examples may be: managed all expenses for five people with enough excess to take an annual vacation; ran two Girls Scout troops simultaneously; created the first children's writers organization and conference in the city; organized a district wide raffle that raised $10,000 for a new library. Make sure your accomplishments are measurable. "Worked on a committee" is not measurable. Example:

<u>2000 to Present</u> — **Organizational and events manager for professional and philanthropic organizations**

> Board member of Planesboro Society of Association Executives —Created communications plan to highlight the benefits of membership that increased membership by 11 percent.
> Western PA Regional Advisor for Society of Writers for Children (SWC)—Created their first annual conference with 240 attendees. Conference Planner SWC Annual Fall Conference —Doubled attendance over two years.
> Newsletter Managing Editor and Planning Committee St. Scholastica Church—Distributed to 300 homes.
> Board member of the Women's Auxiliary of the American Cancer Society—Increased event revenue by 30 percent.
> Writer for Children's Hospital Parent Newsletter sponsored by organization for Children with Special Needs.
> Fundraising and Publicity Committee for Retarded Citizens Association—Event raised $52,500.
> Girl Scouts of Southwestern PA—Brownie, Junior and Cadette Leader running two troops concurrently with forty-two girls.
> Board and Committee Chairman of Lucia's Auxiliary to the Blind Presentation Ball—Event raised $79,000.
> Fundraising Committee for East Shadyside High School—Event raised $42,000.
> Board Member PTG Auxiliary—Reading Enrichment Chairman for O'Malley Elementary School.

3. Under the work experience section on your résumé, if you have not worked outside of the home for several years, list the date or simply the year you began doing these projects. Next to this, place either the date/year you completed them and went back to paid work or state "Present." Example: 1996 to 2006 or 1998 to Present. Underneath this heading list all of the items in 1.
4. Underneath all "Work Experience" entries on your résumé, list a "Key Accomplishments" section and list all the measurable things you accomplished while in each position.
5. Stress your ability to multitask. Anyone who can accomplish all those things while also caring for children exemplifies the transferable skill of organization.

Your age should not be relevant to employment. It is against the law for an interviewer to ask your age or anything regarding children. Of course, you do not want to be defensive about your age either. Just view it as a nonissue. Keep the dates of your education and degrees out of the résumé if you fear age is an issue. Do include dates of work experience.

Avoid using phrases like "responsible for." Instead, use action verbs: "Resolved user problems as part of an Information Technology Department Help Desk serving 1,400 employees."

Always list "Awards and Recognitions" in a separate section of the résumé after the work detail. Include any awards you've been given for work or personal reasons.

Be sure to send a thank you letter to the interviewer. Include what you learned about the company that meshes with your career goals. "I appreciate the opportunity to have seen firsthand that the people of XYZ Corporation are enthusiastic and dedicated to the mission of the company. I would be honored to help them grow that mission."

Again, the most important thing to remember is that employers are looking for people to help them solve problems, not complete tasks. Continue to communicate in the interview, on your résumé and in the thank you letter how you can and have helped to solve problems.

Kevin's Story

Television news casting is where Kevin Sullivan thought he'd spend the life of his career. He had sold his first freelance story to a newspaper at fourteen years old, went on to acquire a degree in journalism and, within three years of graduation, had risen through the ranks of reporting to become news director at a television station in Mississippi. Fast forward eleven years. Kevin was, at the time, executive producer at a station in Birmingham, Alabama, and the climate of the industry had changed.

Over the last decade Kevin had seen an evolution in the news business that led him to become disenchanted with it. Meaningful stories had given way to "What's sexy today?" on the floor of the newsroom. His relationship with his boss was contentious but the thought of changing careers at thirty-six was scary. Eventually, the situation had escalated to intolerable and one day Kevin's biggest fear was realized when he was fired.

Two immediate feelings set—panic and embarrassment. Both of these were met with relief when Kevin began getting phone calls from television markets in other cities. However, after a few of those interviews, he was even more resigned to the fact that he no longer wanted to work in television and he did not want to relocate. Add to that the stress of a marriage that was coming to a close and anxiety became an overwhelming theme in his life. Kevin decided to channel all of his angst into re-crafting a new career path and began that journey by defining his greatest transferable strength.

"I had been a communicator my whole life," said Kevin, who defined very clearly what kind of job he desired. His goal was to take the transferable skill of communications and find a position where he could creatively produce a product of which he was proud. He defined his target industry as public relations, marketing and advertising agencies.

To better chart his path, he sought advice from a company that, for a nominal fee, helped displaced workers find new opportunities. Since Kevin's résumé had previously been drafted for the eyes of television executives, he needed to revise it to highlight his strengths for the fields of PR, marketing and advertising.

Even though there were no positions in these industries in Birmingham, Kevin was able to secure informational interviews that broadened his network of influence. He acquired a mentor during this process that lent him books by top marketing experts such as Jack Trout and others. He read every one and returned them.

However, his job hunt bordered on dismal, forcing Kevin to do a six-month stint as a fast-food manager. Perusing the classifieds one day, he came upon an ad for a marketing director. The industry was not listed in the ad or disclosed in the phone call, but Kevin was determined not to let that deter him and was able to secure an interview.

"I sat in the waiting room surrounded by magazines on trucking and computers and thinking to myself, 'I don't know anything about either one of these,'" said Kevin.

It turned out that the company produced operational software for the trucking industry and was the third largest company of its kind.

Kevin told the president, "I don't know anything about computers or trucking, but I know how to communicate and that is what you need." That line got him hired as their company's first-ever director of marketing. Over the next five years the company grew to become the largest in the industry, showing more than 60 percent growth for three consecutive years and 80 percent in one year.

"I don't take credit for that growth," said Kevin. "I was just part of a team."

Kevin's team player attitude and winning results did not go unnoticed by his company's competitors, one of which offered him a dramatic increase in salary if he'd come to work for them. Kevin's boss said that he couldn't match the offer and told Kevin he'd be crazy not to take it. Kevin left the company on good terms and to this day is still good friends with his former boss.

Six years after first becoming a marketing director, Kevin moved to Atlanta to take a marketing position in the dot.com industry and, six months after moving there, suffered a déjà vu. The company he had been working for folded with little notice and he was left to look for a job, this time in a town where he had not yet built a network of influence. He began interviewing for high tech jobs and was repeatedly told that when the company received its next round of venture funding they'd hire him. There was no telling when that would be, however.

Having lived in other cities, Kevin was familiar with the Book of Lists, an annual ranking of regional businesses in various industries produced by the local business journal. He researched the top public relations firms and wrote each a one-page "pitch" letter, using the skills he had learned from re-crafting his résumé previously.

"The letter focused on how I could help them," said Kevin. "Not how they could help me."

Within a couple of weeks of sending these problem solving letters, Kevin had seven responses and two job offers. He decided to take a position in a large PR firm where he learned the inner workings of a full-scale operation and then transferred those skills to a smaller firm where he could call the shots. There he was able to build the largest book of business the firm ever had. One of his clients was Fisher & Phillips LLP, one of the largest national law firms in the country for labor and employment law with twenty-one offices and 230 attorneys. Fisher & Phillips hired Kevin where, now fifty, he currently serves as their first chief marketing officer in the history of the firm. Unlike the newsroom that he left, Kevin purposefully sought and found employment in companies that fostered collegial cultures, in turn benefiting constituents.

As Kevin looks back on his TV days, he considers being fired a gift.

"They did for me what I didn't have the guts to do," he said, recommending that those in similar positions treat finding new careers as full-time jobs.

Giving back is something Kevin practices regularly. He is actively involved as a volunteer leader in many professional associations where he mentors others.

"Network," he recommends. "Don't make all your efforts about yourself; keep an eye on how you will help others." Kevin never forgot those who helped him through two bouts with unemployment. When he acquired his first position as a marketing director, he contracted for ad agency work with the mentor who had given him those marketing books when he was first unemployed.

"I always remember what he did when I was struggling," said Kevin. "The way my mentor treated me helped me build my confidence that I was on the right path and I would achieve my goal."

Kevin valued and nurtured the relationships he built on his passage and never lost sight of the importance of a positive attitude. "My winding career path has afforded me the opportunity to learn about so many different businesses, ways of life, vocations and ways of thinking that might not have come my way in a more traditional career path."

He advises job seekers to search for companies with a good synergy of service, leadership and people. "A company should be diligently serving its clients, putting customers before profits," said Kevin. "If you do that, the profits will come. A great company also needs leadership, which is ethical and compassionate with a solid moral compass. Service and leadership attract the best employees who will naturally continue to enhance the organization's image."

Remember: List transferable skills you have, which can draw you to a leading opportunity. Write these skills down so that you can articulate them in networking situations.

Exercise #7
From Rule No. 7: Your Résumé is Your Showcase
of Results and Transferable Skills

Identifying Your Transferable Skills:
1. Communication
2. Organizing Information
3. Operating/Fixing Equipment

There are transferable skills that can be applied to any career choice: Your ability to **communicate, organize information** and **operate/fix equipment**. You may be good at instructing others and writing. You may be good at organizing data and keeping records. You may be good at fixing things and making things work. Demonstrate in your résumé your accomplishments in these three areas. Employers know these to be transferable skills. The "Skills" section of your résumé might read: "Highlights of my related skills include:..." Followed by a bullet list of your transferable skills.

How to Determine Your Transferable Skills and Key Accomplishments

Skills from Last Job or Volunteer Work	Transferable - Yes or No?	How Can That Be Used in a New Job?	Related Key Accomplishment
Example: Data entry	Yes	Enter data at any job	Created new format. Result—expanded scope of reports

Chapter Eight

Rule No. 8

Make Your Elevator Speech a Problem Solving Statement

Your opportunities in the job market will be far less abundant than the time you have made available to explore what you want to do and where you want to do it. The same is true for those starting businesses. Once you are open for business, your time for education and professional development will be almost nonexistent. So make good use of this "meanwhile" time by preparing everything you will need when you find your new calling. Your image is important. To build equity in your image, you need to know what services you have to offer that will help people solve problems.

Within the first three seconds of meeting someone, you have made a first impression. People notice the way you are dressed, how you carry yourself, the company you keep, whether or not you are neat, your accessories, your delivery and how you make them feel. They notice whether or not you have common surface denominators. People have a lot to remember and they don't remember what you'd like them to, so they end up storing first impressions in their minds for simplicity's sake. It is virtually impossible to reverse first impressions and it is human nature to hold onto them.

In those first three seconds of your meeting, someone will decide if you are on a comparable professional or social level and draw a judgment as to whether or not s/he wants to further get to know you. If you appear to be of the same or higher status, you are admired and cultivated for further interactions. If you appear to be of lower status, you are tolerated but not targeted to go anywhere from there.

Remember this regarding first impressions: People will forget what you say and do but never how you make them feel.

In an interview situation, you will either appear to fit into the business's culture or not. Your products and services either match the vision of the company with which you are seeking business or they do not. It is that simple.

What you say initially is critically important to people's first impression of you. If you lose them at the beginning, it is basically over before you started. Identifying your image requires self-examination of your own life balance.

> *The Life Balance Self-Examination:* Certain aspects of your life should be in equal balance: family/home, spiritual/ethical, social/cultural, financial/career, mental/educational and physical/health.

This exercise helps identify where the emphasis is in your life. Know full well that this is how other people see you as well. Are you perceived as being in balance? Or are you over-focused on work or athletics? Are you under-focused on spiritual or educational?

Living a balanced life is an ongoing work in progress, but you do not have a lifetime to start over. So make sure that you can definitively describe why someone should hire you, do business with you or refer business to you so that the first impression you give is the one you want.

Liken this description to what you would say if you were fortunate enough to get on the elevator with the president of a company with which you were seeking employment and the president asked you, "So, what do you do?"

Would you say, "Ah, well right now I am looking for a job." I hope not. Because his first impression is that you must not be good at what you do or you would already be doing it for someone else. This response not only doesn't state your accomplishments first, it also doesn't even relay your skills. Ugh!

If you are going for an office manager position, you might say, "I manage front office problems so that executives can solve bigger problems." For the position of financial planner, a statement like this could work: "I help clients live in bigger homes and take better vacations." If you are going for the position of hospital fundraiser, another comment you might make is, "I help to provide services that save lives in the eastern suburbs." For a marketing manager position, you could say, "I create brands that sell products." All of these examples beg the listener to ask, "How do you do that?" This opens the door for more conversation. You could follow the conversation with "Do you have problems in your front office?" or "Have you ever been to Tahiti?"

Rule Break: Don't describe how great you are in your elevator speech. Talk about how you have helped clients solve problems.

How to Write an Elevator Speech:
Take your list of "Key Accomplishments" from the chapter 7: "Your Résumé is Your Showcase of Results and Transferable Skills." Remember that these are ways in which you helped people solve problems. Also note that accomplishments are not skills. If you are an entrepreneur, define all of your globally marketable achievements. Then write two to three sentences that are now your elevator speech. Follow it with what you would say if someone were to ask you, "How do you do that?"

Remember: Make up both a "one minute" elevator speech as well as a "ten second" speech for shorter encounters.

Exercise #8
From Rule No. 8: Make Your Elevator Speech
a Problem Solving Statement

Be Able to Answer "What do you do?" in a
One-Minute Elevator Ride

Use your list of "Key Accomplishments" from exercise 7. Remember that these are ways in which you helped people solve problems. Also remember that accomplishments are not skills. Or if you are an entrepreneur, define all of your globally marketable skills.

How to Write an Elevator Speech:
1. Write down a list of all of your accomplishments. Think of them in terms of how they helped people solve problems. Remember: accomplishments are not skills.

2. Answer the following question: "What is the overall category that encompasses these accomplishments?" Examples: communications (writing, graphic design, photography, art), organization of information (accounting, banking, data entry,) fixing or building things (architect, interior designer, mechanic, information systems support), etc.

    Or

    Simply take your list of "Transferable Skills" from exercise 7.

3. Imagine yourself taking one giant step up the ladder and looking down on this from a higher vantage point. After reviewing the list, write down what overall problem you can solve for people in business. Give just enough information that will beg the question, how do you do that? Is it that you take the headache out of computer systems so that businesses can use their systems to make more money? (Information systems support.) Do you design interior space that draws people to want to hang out there? (Interior designer.) Do you make a company's employees more productive? (Corporate trainer.)

Exercise #8a
From Rule No. 8: Make Your Elevator Speech
a Problem Solving Statement

Personal Accessibility Questionnaire
If you answer "Usually" to these questions, you are leaving a positive impression.

	Usually	Sometimes	Rarely
Do I use the other person's name in a conversation?			
Do I lean toward others when they are speaking, showing interest?			
Do I smile when I meet someone?			
Do I actively invite others to join the conversation and include them?			
Am I well-groomed and comfortable with my appearance?			
Can I hold my eye contact just a little bit longer than others?			
Do I only use positive comments?			
Do I ask questions about my conversational partner as opposed to talking about myself?			
Do I match the depth of what I will personally disclose with that of the conversation?			
Do I laugh at my own mistakes?			
Am I flexible when faced with a challenge?			
Do I share my own vulnerabilities?			
Am I modest and humble about my position and accomplishments?			
Do I take responsibility for my own situation?			
Do I introduce myself to others?			
Am I appropriately playful in my interactions, indicating a comfort level with myself?			
Do I offer to do something for my conversational partner without expecting anything in return?			

Chapter Nine

Rule No. 9

It's Not Who You Know, It's Who Knows You

Every major city has a wide array of business networking opportunities—Rotary, Chamber of Commerce, Kiwanis, Toastmasters, professional associations and other philanthropic organizations. These represent wonderful sources for meeting people in business. Some people seeking employment or new clients attend these meetings, pass out their business cards to as many people as possible and collect equally as many, as if there was a prize at the end of the lunch for the most cards in hand. I encourage you to build relationships, not a telephone list.

Spiritual venues may also serve as good sources to meet people who may have traveled similar journeys to yours. Churches, synagogues, temples, mosques and other religious organizations are comprised of people with callings to spiritual purposes.

You may have other special interests or hobbies that are not as well-known as those listed above but are important to you nonetheless. If you are interested in reading, seek a book club. Or if you are interested in gardening or politics, seek clubs in your area for those interests. All of these may serve as good sources to build relationships.

Small talk is important at any event where you want to meet new people. Aim to spend a maximum of three to five minutes with each person at a lunch meeting or social gathering.

I have always been a person who has enjoyed meeting and talking with people. It has been the one skill that has benefited me more than any other. The reason I enjoy people is that there is so much to learn from others' experiences. As a newspaper reporter, I never had a problem coming up with questions to ask on an interview, because the questions were things that truly drew my curiosity. As a salesperson, I knew that getting to know a client was as easy as asking the client questions about what was important to them. As a professional fundraiser, I knew that engaging donors was a process whereby I listened to them tell their stories about our services. I would then lace through that conversation information on our services they may not have known but was relative to their interests.

You are not building a network of contacts, but you are building a circle of friends. Just listen to what people have to say and you will enlarge that circle.

Acquiring a genuine interest in people will only serve to enhance every area of your life. Why? Because people are the greatest resource for information and their journeys are fascinating. If you have captured the hearts of others with sincere interest in them, their advice can save you from making mistakes and guide you on a clearer course. However, you need to be able to make good judgments on whose advice you will follow.

Even negative advice can be a learning tool. When you listen to someone complain, you can almost feel a sense of dissatisfaction in his or her heart. Did you ever wonder what events of a person's past led up to that feeling? When you hear someone criticize another, you can nearly sense the hurt in the individual's voice. Has he or she not been able to reconcile forgiveness? What would that take? And how do you keep from being paralyzed from similar feelings? Talking with others makes you think about your own situation.

Other people's stories are an important part of meaningful conversations and relationships. If I am ever at a loss as to what to talk about, I always ask a person to tell me about something that happened to them or to someone who they care about. Your genuine interest in these stories will result in the beginning of a trusting relationship, which can lead to a more enriched life for all of us.

Rule Break: Don't just network—connect. Traditional clubs and organizations are good sources for meeting people with similar interests. But I feel that everything you do every day presents an opportunity to meet people who may be part of your new journey. When you are standing in line at the coffee shop, the person in front of you or behind you may have a background similar to your own and may have built a successful empire. A person in your workplace cafeteria may have dealt with challenges similar to yours, but you never knew it. How do you get to know these things about people? Genuinely show an interest in them. When they hear your name you don't want them to say, "I've met her." You want them to say, "I know her." This kind of relationship will come from listening and asking questions, not talking.

How to Make the Most of a Networking Event:
1. Local newspapers generally have lists of various types of meetings throughout the week or month. Familiarize yourself with their lists and review them weekly. Most cities have a weekly business newspaper. Often these events are listed toward the back of the publication. Networking and business opportunities are also listed online. Search on the name of your city and "business calendar" or your special interest.
2. Look for events with topics that interest you where you can meet people from whom you can learn. Review the attendee list ahead of time if possible. If it is handed out at the event, scan it to prioritize those you want to meet.
3. Be there when the event begins. Most of the socializing occurs at the beginning of these events. Introduce yourself with a solid handshake. Repeat their names for your own memory purposes. "Hello, Jack Tracey. It is nice to meet you." The sweetest sound to people's ears is the sound of their own name. The guest speaker will generally follow the networking portion of these events.
4. Make sure you wear your name tag on the right side so that when shaking hands, people can see it prominently. If you have the opportunity to handwrite your name tag, write your first name larger than your last name so that people can see and remember it. Some people put something on the name tag that will inspire people to ask them about it, such as the city where you were born, your nickname, favorite pastime, number or magazine. Try to tie this in with the theme of the event. You may be at a Chamber of Commerce meeting on a local amusement tax. You may write down your favorite ride at the local amusement park. Don't write the name of the company for which you work, write what you do. You don't work for a hospital— you help doctors save lives. These points will help spark conversation. Conversation starters are the first part of relationship building.

5. Drop the "What's in it for me" perspective. You are there to offer to help others solve problems and build relationships. It's all about them.
6. Have plenty of business cards. When you take someone else's business card, be sure to have a special place to put it. Some people give their cards out from the right pocket of their suit jacket while collecting those of others in their left pocket. Do not ever write on somebody's business card in front of them. You want them to know that you value that card. (You wouldn't write on an award someone had just given you.)
7. Don't dismiss people because you think they may not be able to help you. Chances are they know a person who can.
8. Make sure that first you offer something to the person you meet before you ask for advice, a referral, his or her time or anything back.

Eight-Step Process to Connect with Someone New:
1. *Define what you want to be known as.* What is your personal brand? What is the message you send—and your audience receives—about you? Do you want to be known as a problem solver, an expert, a philanthropist? Creative? Aggressive? Dynamic or Disciplined?
2. *Pay a compliment.* A compliment immediately grabs attention. Who doesn't want to hear something good about themselves? It also softens the response of the person receiving the compliment, often making that individual smile and can open the door to a conversation. "You showed excellent patience." "You have a wonderful sense of style." "You don't know me, but I read about your company's latest acquisition of 'X' company and the marrying of the two corporations will better position you in the market. Congratulations."
3. *Ask a question.* The good thing about a question is that it leaves the conversation in the other person's control and takes the angst off you. "I've never had that flavor of coffee. How does it compare to the Columbian?" Follow your first question with another until the conversation gets rolling. At a networking meeting you might ask, "What brought you here today?"
4. *Say something funny—if you are funny.* If you are standing in line at a place or meeting, it can be boring and tedious. A funny comment will lessen the tension for others near you. Humor is most effective when it is not at anyone's expense, when you poke fun at yourself and when your comments are leading in one direction and you say

something unexpected. "I love to get coffee here so that I can share the experience with lots of people of overpaying for hot water being poured over beans."

5. *Offer to do something for them.* People are generally awed by a stranger who offers to do them favors. "I have a good article on that in my office. If you give me your card, I will be happy to forward it to you." "I live near there. Let me pick it up for you and I'll give it to you tomorrow when I see you here."

6. *Send the person something unexpected that relates to something you talked about during a brief encounter.* If you met at a meeting, make note of something he or she is interested in and send the person something that he or she will find helpful or valuable, such as an article on a relevant subject, a clipping you saw that featured that person in a newspaper or publication or a simple greeting card for a special occasion.

7. *Ask questions and listen.* People always want to talk about themselves. Show interest in something they have done and ask them how they did it. A person's name tag might be a great place to start a conversation. What does your company do? What was your biggest obstacle along the way? How did they manage their time? You will learn valuable insight and show the person that you are genuinely interested in what s/he is doing. This will in turn endear the person to your genuine interest. Always include everyone in a conversation. Others nearby will appreciate your gratuitousness.

8. *End graciously.* To end a conversation and move onto the next person you would like to meet, simply say, "It was a pleasure meeting you; perhaps we could talk again sometime about software," or "It was very nice to meet you and I look forward to hearing more about your business. May I call you sometime next week?" and depart.

Remember: Send the person you just met at an event or meeting something that you think might interest him or her.

Exercise #9
From Rule No. 9: It's Not Who You Know, It's Who Knows You

Establishing Your Network of Friends

1. How important is networking to you? ❏ Vital   ❏ Important   ❏ Useful   ❏ Not

2. At least how often do you attend networking events?
   ❏ At least once a month   ❏ At least every 2-3 months
   ❏ At least 4-6 months   ❏ Less often

3. Your Key Contacts

Networking Category	Name(s)	Key Benefits for Them & Me
Family		
Friends		
Current Colleagues		
Former Colleagues		
Colleagues Outside the Organization		
Hobby Friends		
Social Activities		
Community Friends		
Professional Associations		
Government		
Volunteer Activities		
Alumni		
Customers		

Chapter Ten

Rule No. 10

SMART Five- and Ten-Year
Goals That Rock

Yes, this part is scary. Nobody likes to set goals. Why? Because if you set a goal, you run the risk of failing to meet it. And nobody wants to feel as if he or she is a failure. So, most people feel safer not setting goals. Keep one thing in mind. Most people also do not end up successful, either.

However, if you do not set goals, you will not achieve your potential, because you will not have direction. You need to have specific measurable goals written down and you need to review them often. The payoff is how you will feel when you achieve them.

Think about your future in a new way with this question:

What would you attempt to do if you knew you could not fail?

My oldest friend gave me a paperweight with these words on it that I look at on my desk every day. Fears are a deterrent to goals. Practice ignoring them.

Your work, your relationships with people, your outside activities— they are all like boats at a dock. You will all have the opportunity some day to get in one. And the boat will start to pull away from the pier. If you have a set of oars, you will drive the boat. If you don't, the boat will drive you. You probably won't sink, but you will probably find yourself circling the inlet for a very long time, never pulling out of the harbor for a destination.

In setting goals, remember two key principles: 1) Begin with the End in Mind—Your "Success Sketch" (chapter 1) and 2) It is Important to Fail Early (next chapter).

Have you ever heard people say, "I hate my job" or "I hate that person"? Next time you hear that, even if it is from your own lips, ask the question, "What are your (my) goals to make a change?"

Setting goals are like grabbing hold of the oars in a boat: They are what you must use to steer.

Goal setting is not just for defining what company or profession is right for you. Think about things such as: Do I ultimately want to live around the people I love—my family? Do I like to sail or ski and want to live in a climate that supports these sports? Is my course selection diverse enough so that I can find work in many different fields?

Goals are not notions. They are specific, measurable steps that have a set time frame. "I am going to get that job" is a notion. "I am going to research the company's Web site on Monday, read their annual report Tuesday and contact my network of friends to see if they know anyone inside the company I can talk with on Wednesday" is a goal.

When I graduated from high school, my goal was to get a good job and be able to move to a warmer climate. I went off to a college in Michigan, where I majored in an allied health profession and took a job in the Houston Medical Center upon graduation. Within my first month there I realized I had made a mistake. Houston was a booming and exciting town, but it was not a place I wanted to live for the rest of my life. Yes, it was sunnier than the sixty days of sun per year that Pittsburgh has and it was closer to the ocean, but I had taken for granted things that were truly important, because I had never experienced life without them. I wanted to be around family. I enjoyed the multi-cultural aspects of an old eastern city. I enjoyed the character of old neighborhoods and I missed the short commute it took to get around a smaller city.

I did, however, realize that in the Houston Medical Center I could gain valuable work experience that I couldn't get in any other part of the world. So while in Houston, I concentrated on placing myself in excellent work situations that would give me experience that I could not get elsewhere. I really didn't want to fall in love and marry someone and have to live there the rest of my life so I set a goal: I would work in Houston for two years (specific goal with a timeframe) and then I would move to a place where my professional experience would stand out (keeping the end in mind).

After exactly two years, I moved back to Pittsburgh. Sure, while in Houston I had to focus on smaller goals such as where I wanted to live, what kind of furniture I'd buy and what kind of car I would drive. I spent many weekends crabbing in Seabrook and on the beaches in Galveston as well. However, the ultimate place I wanted to be was back in Pittsburgh with great work experience behind me.

Once I had moved back to Pittsburgh, I set another goal: In two years I would buy a house. Well, I hadn't figured on falling in love, marrying and buying a house with my husband. I continued to work in my profession before our oldest daughter was born. However, I was beginning to see that while I was very fulfilled in an allied health profession at twenty-five, there really wasn't a lot of room for advancement in that particular field. I couldn't imagine doing the same work at forty-five or even at twenty-six for that matter. I have an entrepreneurial spirit, which breeds restlessness if not channeled into achievement.

As it turned out, I was at a crossroads: I could continue doing allied health work forever. (Remember the people who say they hate their jobs? I saw myself becoming one of them.) Or, I could work at something new, which was risky. I decided that it was better to fail early at my first career choice rather than spend the rest of my life trying to convince myself that I liked it. But now I had to recreate a new career path.

I had always loved unusual gifts from people and could see their place in the corporate world. Soon I started building a corporate gift business on the side while I was working in a large physician's office so that when we started a family in two years, I'd have a home based business in place. This carried a calculated risk that gave me the luxury of a paying job to fall back on while building a business on the side. And I had a measurable time-line—two years. After my daughter was born, I resigned from my full-time position and worked more on the home business, which served us very well until my second daughter, third daughter and son were born and the inventory and time commitment became overwhelming to juggle with family responsibilities. My children were very young and I did not want to leave home to work just yet so I traded in my gift baskets and plastic wrap for my other passion—writing. I had done a lot of writing for organizations for which I was volunteering, so when I saw an ad in the *Pittsburgh Post-Gazette* for freelance writers, I told myself, "I can do that."

It had never dawned on me that I couldn't do this work. I recognized that I had absolutely no formal education as a writer and had absolutely never been paid to write anything. But I had done a lot of writing over the previous five years for children and other organizations in which I had volunteered, so I sent clips of some of those writings to the newspaper.

I had no fear of rejection. What was the worst that could happen? They wouldn't think my work was good enough? So what. That was not the worst thing that had ever happened to me.

When I went for the interview, I'll never forget what the *Post-Gazette* editor told me: "You can write like you are having a conversation around the dining room table. That's what we look for." So at this point, I had pretty much realized that I was not going back to the profession in which I had a degree. Soon I was writing five stories a week for the newspaper, had picked up a lot of other freelance work such as the public relations director of a public school district and became the executive director of a trade association—all of this was work I did from home.

"I am trying" is not a specific or measurable goal.

"I will do it in this amount of time" is.

If you knew that finances, family, location and any other practical responsibility could not get in the way of what you ultimately wanted, where would you see yourself? Think about the things that you enjoyed doing as a child, but never had the time to develop. Think about friends and family—are they in your plan?

Ask yourself, "Who and what is driving me?"

Rule Break: If setting goals scares you, then don't set goals. Dream! Take a blanket out to the backyard, lie down in the grass, stare up at the sky and dream. Let nothing get in the way. See no barriers. Think of everything you ever wanted to do and still haven't done. What feels good? Remember what you dreamed about as a child. What have you always wanted to do?

A Good Goal is a SMART Goal:

S – SPECIFIC

M - MEASURABLE

A - ACHIEVABLE (but challenging)

R - RESULTS ORIENTED

T - TIME FRAMED

"I want to make more money (sell more, have more time)" does not cut it as a short-term goal. Consider instead:

I will increase my salary/draw by $XX by June 2XXX.

I will grow my customer base from X to Y by year's end.

I will write down three processes per month so that I can delegate these to others.

I will generate $XX in revenue and $XX in profit in 2XXX by setting monthly goals.

I will hold a team meeting each month throughout 2XXX with measurable expectations for each team member.

I will lose ten pounds in three months by working out for thirty minutes four days per week so I can improve my overall health.

It is important to write down your goals and check them often. This gives you the opportunity to remember them and modify them if need be over time. You may also alter your "Success Sketch" based on your five- and ten-year plan.

The fact is that as you continue to see yourself in your plan, you are more likely to stay on course to get there.

Writing your goals down on paper solidifies your thinking and sets the direction for your brain to accomplish them. Start with small goals. Achieving smaller goals will give you the motivation to tackle more complex goals.

Once you've established five- and ten-year goals you will start to see the short-range strategies you need to get there. Develop strategies or actions you will implement over the next sixty to ninety days to move you closer to your goal. Don't start with too many steps. Begin with a few and add more or modify them as you complete the tasks.

Again, goals are not notions. I often tell my children, "I will get an 'A'" is not a goal. Good goals are specific, measurable and have a time frame for the result. "I will reread the chapter Monday, take the practice test Tuesday and reread my notes Wednesday" is a good goal.

Finally, celebrate your wins along the way! Take the time to reward yourself for the little accomplishments since these will lead to bigger successes down the road. Stop and get yourself a gourmet cup of coffee. Make it a point to call a friend for lunch. Put the leash on the dog and take an informal tour of all the summer gardens in your neighborhood.

Drew's Story

At thirty-eight, Drew Stevens had just flown home to St. Louis, Missouri, with his wife after his mother-in-law's funeral to discover a package at the front door indicating that he had been terminated. The very financial services company for which he had relocated just ten months prior fired him. After several weeks of being unemployed, the CEO of a global billion dollar firm gave him a job as Director of Sales. But his trials were not over. Drew found out within a few months that he, the CEO and his wife (who worked at the firm) were fired. Then he took a position with another financial services firm, again to be fired for the third time—this time on Christmas Eve by a friend of his.

Stress and great challenge were not strangers to Drew. As a child he grew up in an abusive home and was kicked out of the house at fifteen. Throughout his life he came to realize two things that he believes are the keys to ultimate success: 1) know how to think and act independently and 2) know how to adapt in stressful situations by setting goals.

A neighbor suggested that it might be a good idea for Drew to be a teacher. After all, he had an MBA and a Ph.D. in Organization and Management. In addition, Drew was already an adjunct instructor at one small university. Drew saw it as a good suggestion and began studying corporate training and development materials. He spotted an advertisement in the back of a magazine with the headline "Speak now. Speak often. And use your own words." For $150, he ordered the books and set up a Web site to market his training services.

Within six weeks of developing the site, Drew was asked to be the keynote speaker at an event for international sales professionals, which led to an all expenses paid trip to Johannesburg, South Africa.

"Failure is education," said Drew. "Look at failure as an opportunity to take it to another level."

For the first two years, Drew juggled his training business with other part-time work. After all, he had a mortgage, two automobile payments and a family to support. He began by traveling around the country doing speaking engagements for $200 a day until eventually he realized he was creating a lot of angst and not a lot of income. He also was missing precious time with his wife and two children.

"I was letting the business run me," said Drew, who remembers calling home one night from out of town to hear his four-and-a-half-year-old son say, "I am used to kissing one parent good night."

It was then that Drew realized that he needed to be much more than a speaker. He set goals so that his speaking engagements would give him opportunities for consulting and so his consulting engagements would give him opportunities to speak. This plan developed multiple products, which he sells online, that has established passive income.

"I was too 'siloed' in looking at niche areas of my business," admits Drew. He knew similar to corporate businesses, he needed diversification to help with the ebbs and flows of clients' needs. Drew's ultimate goal was to create a million dollar business with no employees that his children could take over or sell.

Today Drew travels far less. His company, Stevens Consulting Group, has harmonized his speaking and consulting services as well as his products around a successful sales methodology. His "process training" helps selling professionals become strategists instead of tacticians. Products include books, e-books and audio products.

"Successful entrepreneurs know what they want and remain focused on the goal," said Drew. His only regret is that he didn't start sooner or seek good mentors early on. Now he enjoys mentoring people in his business every day.

"Never say, 'should've, would've, could've,'" he advises.

Remember: Set goals to get to your success sketch.

Exercise #10
From Rule No. 10: *SMART* Five and Ten-Year Goals That Rock

Five-Year and Ten-Year Goal Plan

It is important to understand that where you are in five years probably is not where you want to be in ten years. Center your decision making on strategies that will get you where you want to be. Decisions you make today should be channeled toward your goals. Make sure the goals are **S**pecific, **M**easurable, **A**chievable, **R**esults Centered within a **T**ime Frame.

Reevaluate these goals annually.

Questions	In Five Years	In Ten Years
Where are your family members living and how old will they be?		
Are you in the same job or line of work?		
Is travel involved?		
Where will you be living?		
What will your average day look like?		
What will your place of residence look like and how close is it to being paid off?		
How close will you be to paying off other loans? School? Car? Business?		
What is the status of your retirement plan?		
What interests or sports have you not had time to develop that interest you?		
How does volunteerism figure into the picture?		
Is a business part of the picture?		

Exercise #10a
From Rule No. 10: *SMART* Five- and Ten-Year Goals That Rock

Professional Development Worksheet

1. Do a Personal SWOT Analysis:

   a) What are your STRENGTHS? What are you good at, recognized for, proud of?

   b) What are your WEAKNESSES? What is hard, holds you back, has you vulnerable?

   c) What are your OPPORTUNITIES? Can you optimize strengths, develop potential?

   d) What are your THREATS? What setbacks do you anticipate?

2. Define a Career Mission Statement:
   This is your long-term vision of where you want to be—five years at least. It is your purpose. Try to keep it to ten words. Think about what values lead you in that direction. Example: I will continue to learn management strategies and be an executive director by the time I am forty-five.

3. Major Career Objectives: (The steps that will accomplish your mission.)
   Use the SMART strategies for setting goals from chapter 10 to define the steps that will get you to your mission. When and where will you get more education if you need it? Do you need to change where you work—by when? How will you master a skill you don't have?

Objectives That Will Get Me to My Mission	To be Accomplished When?	To be Accomplished Where?
1.		
2.		
3.		
4.		

Chapter Eleven

Rule No. 11

It is Important to Fail Early

In the previous chapter we discussed that when you are setting goals, you must remember two things: 1) Begin with the end in mind and 2) It is important to fail early.

No one begins a new venture and expects to fail. The reality is that more businesses, relationships and ventures fail than become successful. The Girl Scout and Boy Scout motto will serve you well here: "Be prepared." That way, if you fall short on your goals, you can move onto something that WILL succeed before you completely fall down the *chute*.

The challenging part of taking calculated risks is recognizing early that what you are doing is not working, which is a very difficult task indeed. Imagine that you have just moved to a new community where you don't know anybody and have taken on the volunteer task of putting together a community directory. You put information forms in every mailbox and communicate to the neighborhood that your goal is to help older residents be able to contact homes with teenagers for yard work. Your hope is that families with children can get to know one another and that new camaraderie might result in someone organizing a summer block party. Then, as you are putting the directory together, you realize that the dynamic of the community has not lent itself to meet your goal. Older residents begin calling you to help them find someone to shovel their snow and neighbors are asking you when the block party is. At this point, it's time to appreciate that the directory has provided a good service to help neighbors get to know one another and has also assisted you in meeting wonderful new friends in the process. However, it may be time to step out of the forefront of this process so that you may set other rewarding goals to help others and yourself.

Be ready to take risks—calculated risks. It is wiser to fail early rather than do nothing and remain safe.

As I was analyzing what I could do to best support my children in a way that would make me happy, I realized very quickly that my degreed profession was not going to gratify me for the rest of my life, nor would it provide a decent wage. So I experimented in things that I enjoyed— writing, desktop publishing, leading, sales, fundraising and management. I sought things for which I could set measurable goals that would satisfy my desire to guide others, be creative and make a difference in the world. I didn't want to be someone who complained that she hated her job. It was within my control to choose another job, another profession or another division within the corporation.

If you see that results are coming in later than expected but are consistently rising to your expectations, just a little later than you anticipated, this means that you are probably okay. If you see that you are having a hard time getting to the steps on your timeline but the results are progressively consistent, you are at least moving in a positive direction. You may just need to adjust the timelines.

If you see that you are able to execute your steps in a timely manner but the results are not occurring on your timeline nor improving, then you might want to reconsider strategy or "get out." Don't deny the trends.

Consider Jake, who wanted to quit his job as a waiter to start an eBay store online selling treasures he found at garage sales. He set a timeline over nine months that included setting up an account with PayPal, setting up his Web site and eBay store, selecting the right camera to photograph his merchandise, acquiring merchandise to sell, defining the best shipping method and acquiring shipping materials and determining the average profit per piece than he expected to have earned at the end of nine months. What he found is that the profit per piece was less than he expected, but it was a good supplemental income. He decided to keep his online business on the side, as he loves garage sales, but not quit his job as a waiter. He now knows that if he wants to ultimately quit his job, he will need to find another line of work or business that is more lucrative. He found online selling rewarding and investigates other new products to sell online that do not take as much time to acquire as garage sale items. He created a timeline for this process as well.

Think about Gail, an unhappy woman whose goal was to have a happy and fulfilling marriage. She wanted to give her marriage every opportunity to do so but did not want to spend the rest of her life in misery if it couldn't. She set up a timeline over six months with written STEPS that included speaking with her pastor, arranging for marital counseling, going to counseling and scheduling weekly nights out with her husband. Her anticipated RESULTS that correlate with these steps were to gain better peace, have regular appointments for counseling sessions, to learn better communication strategies from the counselor and to begin to enjoy spending time together again. Two months into marital counseling the counselor concluded that there was a lack of respect in the relationship. Gail had arranged one date with her husband, but she felt as if she were dining alone. Her pastor advised her to seek personal counseling on her own, which she did. Yet at the end of the six months she hasn't come anywhere close to executing the STEPS let alone gaining the RESULTS.

It is hard to deny facts that are on paper. You can justify a lot in your mind but objective measurable data on paper is hard to argue.

Rule Break: As you continue to see yourself in a successful light by getting closer to your "Success Sketch", don't let that shield you from practical planning. Identify possible pitfalls to your success early. Alerting yourself to the signs of potential pitfalls can show you when to get out or modify your plans. You will not dwell on the pitfalls, but the pitfalls will be a measurable outcome in tracking the timeline of your success.

Failing early might also mean redirecting your steps toward something more attainable, albeit in the same realm as your original goal. It is all about taking risks—calculated risks. Be fearless, not reckless.

Famous People Who Have Failed:
1. He was fired from a newspaper for his lack of imagination and original ideas—Walt Disney.
2. She was dismissed from acting school with a note that said she was too shy—Lucille Ball.
3. He was a failed military soldier, farmer and real estate agent who, at thirty-eight years old, went to work for his father as a handyman—Ulysses S. Grant.

4. He was cut from his high school basketball team, went home, locked himself in his room and cried—Michael Jordan.
5. He failed in business twice, had a nervous breakdown and was defeated in eight elections—Abraham Lincoln.
6. His teacher told him he was too stupid to learn anything and that he should go into a field that emphasized his pleasant personality—Thomas Edison.
7. They were turned down by a recording company and told guitar music was on the way out—The Beatles.

Remember: Even the most famous people in the world didn't get to where they are in life without a few speed bumps along the way!

Exercise #11
From Rule No. 11: It is Important to Fail Early

Three Steps to Create a "Go or Get Out" Timeline

Before you begin a project, set a specific project GOAL of what you want to accomplish. Create a timeline that will lead to that goal by creating four columns on a piece of paper with the goal written at the top. In column one, write the DATE. In column two, write the STEPS that will lead to your goal. In column three, write the RESULTS that you expect after you execute each specific step. And in column four write WHEN for what week or month you expect each result to occur. As you analyze this over the next several weeks and months you will be able to see trends that will help you better understand if your anticipated plan is working. Don't deny the trends. If you have accomplished the STEP within a reasonable time frame but results aren't coming, you may want to adjust the WHEN. If you aren't even close, it may be time to rethink the GOAL and/or the STEPS.

My GOAL for this project is: _____

Example: I will start a small business as a freelance virtual assistant in three months.

DATE Started	STEPS to Get There	RESULTS I Expect	WHEN I Expect Them
Example: January 14th	*I will find a mentor by searching the Internet via message boards and groups to find one.*	*Expect to find one.*	*Within one month.*

Exercise #11a
From Rule No. 11: It is Important to Fail Early

The Life Plan Assessment

The following questions are to help you decide if you are on the right course to reach your short and long-term goals. The more "yes" answers you have the more balanced your life is and the more opportunities you will have. If you see a pattern emerge you know that you are either on the right course or you need to make some changes. To make changes, reevaluate and review your goals.

Assessment Questions	Yes	No
When you get up in the morning are you excited about what you are doing?		
Is your work solving problems and making a difference?		
Are your daily tasks challenging you to think outside of the box and allowing you to be creative?		
Do you feel that you are in the right department within the organization?		
Does current management acknowledge your worth within the organization—especially regarding attitude and productivity?		
Is there room for you to advance within the organization?		
Are you making time away from work to be with the people with whom you are close?		
Have you developed a circle of relationships that is rewarding to you?		
Do you have the opportunity to learn new things and advance your knowledge base for new opportunities?		
Are you helping to train others?		
Are you involved in team building and conflict resolution?		
Have you found mentors inside and outside of the office?		
Are you mentoring someone yourself?		
Are you asking for more responsibility?		
Are you suggesting ideas to help advance the mission of the organization?		
Are you able to balance work with your health and outside interests?		
Are you developing relationships with leaders within the organization?		
Are you able to avoid confrontations?		
Can you respond to perceived threats without being defensive?		
Do you not criticize others? If you are, then what do you need to change?		
Are you patient with yourself?		
Are you patient with others?		
Do you compliment others?		
Do you treat others with respect, even when referring to them if they are not present? If not, what do you need to change?		
Do you show a personal interest in your co-workers?		
Do you show a regular personal interest in the people you are close to?		
Do you have your success sketch of where you want to be posted where you can see it every day?		

Chapter Twelve

Rule No. 12

Help Yourself by
Helping Others First

In earlier chapters on finding a mentor and networking, I commented that helping others will always bring you more than you give away. Consider helping others in ways that are not just professional to open your mind to new possibilities.

Volunteering is truly a selfless effort that will do as much or more for you than those you serve. Many people who become successful find that they have time to give back and volunteer their efforts for very worthwhile causes. They are often recognized at fancy dinners where they are honored for their outstanding service. Most of the time they will tell you, and I have learned this as well, that you get more reward from volunteering than you feel you gave to the cause. It is a privilege to help others. Again, the Girl Scouts have it right, "...make the world a better place."

You are probably saying to yourself, "I don't have time to hold my life together as it is. How am I going to volunteer?" This is the same thing I said to myself when I was at a truly low point in my life. I could barely support my children, was not sure if we'd have a place to live or medical care and couldn't see the light at the end of the tunnel. At that time I was a Girl Scout leader of two troops and I thought I was doing enough to guide my children and give back. Then, one Sunday at church, I saw an advertisement on the bulletin board for people to help put meals together for the homeless after mass. I took my children along and, as a family, we found it an honor to do this small service. It got the focus off us and onto those who needed it more. This short activity snapped me out of my doldrums and back to reality.

I went on to do this volunteer work one evening a week until my job schedule did not permit it. This small act of giving did much more for me than it did for the people it served. I saw a lot more people out there who were much worse off than I was. I continue to do community service on a regular basis, serving on boards for non-profit organizations and giving classes to community groups for people trying to start their lives over.

On Christmas Day, the children and I have made it a tradition to deliver poinsettias provided by the generosity of donors to patients at the Forbes Regional Hospital in Pittsburgh. Doing this has truly become a special privilege. Discussions about what lavish gifts friends had received come to screeching halts when you see a family eating their Christmas dinner at the bedside of a sick loved one. It kind of puts it all in perspective.

As a professional fundraiser, I have seen the value of philanthropy and what it can do to instill values and meaning in a family. One need not be wealthy to be charitable. I am truly inspired every year when we execute an employee campaign at my hospital and I see some of the lowest paid employees donating an hour of pay per month so that family members of dying loved ones in our hospice program may have respite care or family members on the oncology floor will have a resource library.

Even at my lowest points, I always made an effort to contribute to my church, the Salvation Army kettles and other meaningful causes. I didn't have much, but I could always find something for those less fortunate, because indeed there were many of them out there.

The spirit of giving is contagious. What you do now is observed and copied by others around you. Today I watch my children, who are poor college kids, take change from their wallets to put in the same kettles they watched me give to over the years.

There's an old saying regarding the impact of philanthropy on maintaining family values and wealth: "From shirtsleeves to shirtsleeves in three generations." Not surprisingly, this phrase became popular during the "Robber Baron" era of the 1870s and 1880s when poor immigrants, such as Andrew Carnegie and John D. Rockefeller, arrived in an industrial town, rolled up their sleeves and developed endless prosperity laboring relentlessly with elements such as coal and coke.

Once they'd acquired their fortunes, both Carnegie and Rockefeller spent the rest of their lives dispersing it in medical, educational and other philanthropic institutions, which, to this day, are towering testaments to their families.

John D. Rockefeller's advice to his children was to give 10 percent of their income to charity, save 10 percent and have fun spending the rest.

But many figures of the Robber Baron age who made immense fortunes were not of a generous or philanthropic nature and handed the money on as a life belt to their children who then squandered it, so much so that the next generation had returned to the shirtsleeves in which their grandfathers had landed in the United States.

Hence the phrase: "From shirtsleeves to shirtsleeves in three generations."

There is a stunningly high failure rate that follows the transition of wealth to heirs. This is a worldwide phenomenon that hovers around the 70 percent level.

Financial planners today counsel clients on the value of philanthropy, a family mission and planning to insure that family wealth continues to touch further generations of the family. Yet such planning is not only for the wealthy. Instilling the value of caring for others and maintaining a generous spirit diminishes the potential of selfishness.

Philanthropy is one of the major ties that bind families together both emotionally and financially over generations by teaching financial stewardship and the preservation of family values.

I try to put this philosophy to work within my own family, which evolves less like the Carnegies and more like the Family Circus. While still in college and high school, I have explained the "From shirtsleeves to shirtsleeves" phenomenon to my four children. Every Christmas one of their gifts is a monetary one for which they are to select a favorite charity to be the beneficiary of a donation of that amount in their name. At first they were quick to tell me that we are not wealthy, did not need to worry about selfish squandering and that they should donate the money to themselves. Sigh...

However, over time, the children have found fun in researching a favorite charity or cause on the Internet. Most of the causes are centered on children—a good connection to their own lives. All of the children have done countless hours of volunteer service, which has led them to pursue careers and activities of service.

The average person finds it hard to make the time to volunteer. I say make time to volunteer—even if it is an hour or two a week—because in this selfless act, you will find what really matters in life. What you will see and feel will be new and help you get used to new feelings as you travel this journey to a new place. Recognition is insignificant. You don't need lavish award dinners to feel good about what you are doing, because you are not doing this to be seen—you are doing it to help others and nurture your soul.

Volunteering becomes doubly important if you are not sure what career path to take. The exposure to different professions and social services will help you narrow your interests and pinpoint where you really want to spend your time. It will help you define what your talents are and in what areas you need to develop more skills. Volunteering will teach you the discipline of working a certain schedule and being account-able to others. It will help new people get to know you.

In my mid-thirties, when I was trying to reenter the work force, I was juggling multiple projects. I was freelance writing four to five stories a week for the largest newspaper in town, was the executive director of a trade asso-ciation, was the part-time public relations director of a public school district and did freelance writing and graphic design for a number of small busi-nesses—all work I did from home. A special education teacher in the public school district for which I was the PR director asked me if I would help her obtain a grant for a summer program for the special education students. She explained to me the sad truth of how they regressed over the summer and needed the structure and predictability of a routine to keep up their skill growth. I wanted to help her. I didn't know how to do that, but I told her I would. The only fundraising I had ever done was volunteering to help with balls, fashion shows, plays and the like.

I went to the Foundation Center of the local library and signed up for every class they had on grant writing. I spent time in the library studying grants, funders and the process. I called dozens of foundations seeking guidance and most of them were very helpful in steering me in the right direction. I taught myself how to write a grant proposal and even got an appointment with the local community foundation. At that appointment, I opened the presentation with a long, prepared speech and learned very quickly that my presence at that meeting was of least importance and that the teacher, principal and superintendent were key. So, after that, I kept my mouth shut and lateraled the ball to the key players who caught and ran well with it. This taught me that I better prepare the key players instead of myself next time. Everything is a learning experience.

At that point, we were successful at obtaining a $68,000 grant for this special education program, which served the students very well. The district agreed to continue the program after the funding cycle as a result of its impact on the students. I never got paid for acquiring that grant. And I never asked to be paid. I earned way more than a monetary reward. I learned how to do something of value that people need—I learned how to raise money.

After we obtained this grant, we went on to acquire $450,000 to rehabilitate and install lights on their athletic field. This was not as compelling of a case for support as educating special needs children, so I knew this would be more difficult. But I mentored under a school board member who was a master networker. He wisely identified state funds as a source for this project and engaged the state legislator who served the district to get behind the project. This school board member was very supportive of this legislator and was willing to use his sphere of influence to better his district. He also identified key individual donor prospects and offered naming opportunities to them so they could build their legacy in the community. It all fell into place like a perfectly orchestrated symphony. In the end, we were able to get a state grant for $450,000, a donor to name the stadium and other donors to name the locker rooms, equipment rooms and more. It wasn't my ability to draft the grant proposal or other documents that secured the money, although it was a necessary and tedious part of the process. It was the relationships grown out of networking that sealed the deals. That is where I truly learned that networking was about understanding the needs of others and helping them achieve their goals.

I never got paid for working on that grant, either. Again, I never asked to be paid. In fact, I should have paid them. I wouldn't be where I am today if I hadn't had the opportunity to learn a new skill while making a meaningful difference in this capacity. When I retired from this PR position to take my first full-time position as a professional fundraiser, the district had the state issue a citation award to me in appreciation for helping them to raise $518,000. The experience was invaluable and one I'd have never gotten if I had not offered to do the work on a volunteer basis. Shortly after this and when my youngest child was in school full-time, I took that citation on an interview for a job as the executive director of a hospital foundation in charge of all of the hospital's fundraising.

I had never worked as a professional fundraiser. The job was not to be the major gifts officer, event planner, vice president of operations or any of the other myriads of jobs in the fundraising profession. This was the lead job for which I did, in fact, receive the offer because what I had raised in a short period of time—$518,000 on my first two attempts to fundraise—was more than they had raised in a year. Not to mention, this was specific, measurable and done within a finite time frame.

I was with that hospital for two years and was then offered the position at a larger hospital as president and CEO of their Foundation with twenty-five million dollars in assets. Our capital campaign goal was five million dollars over two years. We raised $10.4 million in two years.

Rule Break: Your local hospital and animal shelter, especially in these difficult times, certainly are seeking volunteers because of the large number of constituents that they serve. There is something comforting about volunteering at a place that you know has such an impact in your community. Consider reaching out and exploring volunteering at a place you have not yet visited, but is of interest to you. Try volunteering on a grassroots level at a place that is very low profile, but serves a real need in the community. It will teach you how to stretch out of your comfort zone, which will help you do the same in other areas as well. Non-profits always need help with special events in order to advance their mission. I say volunteer on the level of the people they are raising money to support. If you have always had an interest in children, ask if you may host a story hour and read at your local library. If your interest is more in the arts, ask if you may help a non-profit set up an art show. If you care about women's issues, contact your local women's shelters or universities that hold classes on going back to work and see if you may become involved in the care or education of women in crisis. If your time is limited ask if there is something you can do from home to help.

Organizations That Can Benefit from Your Volunteer Service:
1. Homeless Shelters
2. Food Banks
3. Girl Scouts and Boy Scouts
4. Special Olympics
5. Habitat for Humanity
6. Your Local Church
7. State Parks
8. City Programs for Youth and Others
9. Big Brother/Big Sister
10. Hospitals
11. Libraries
12. Senior Centers
13. Animal Shelters
14. United Way

15. Red Cross
16. Salvation Army
17. Environmental Organizations

And many others. Just think of the things that interest you. There is surely a non-profit organization that needs your time.

You may love to take photographs, decorate your house, entertain and read. You may be good at organizing things, communicating with people and juggling multiple tasks. A women's shelter may benefit from your decorating ability or a food pantry may benefit from a canned goods drive you could organize.

You don't need to be a certified expert to help people. You need to care about others and want to help them. If you love children and love to golf, you could host a free golf clinic at a local Boys and Girls Club. If you are a good cook and are well-organized, you may want to give a free cooking demonstration at your local community center. If you have a nice voice and like to meet people, you may volunteer to answer the phone at a local service agency.

Whatever volunteer work you choose to do, make sure that you prepare. If you are giving a demonstration, plan it and have handouts. If you are volunteering at an animal shelter, does it need blankets? Practice what you will be doing ahead of time. Your children often make a great audience.

Tawnya's Story

At age thirty-one, Tawnya Sutherland was teaching classes in artistic rubber stamping as well as selling stamp products in eastern Canada when she sold her business and moved with her husband and three children to Ontario. Within one year of moving 3,500 miles away from her friends and family for her husband's job, Tawnya found herself divorced and a single parent of three children under eleven years old.

"Panic set in," said Tawnya. "I felt the whole world was falling apart."

Tawnya and her husband had previously set up a business together where she had done bookkeeping and secretarial work. So she put those skills to good use and took a job as a vice president for a computer service company for six months. The demands of the job grew to consume up to twelve hours of her day, making child care cost prohibitive and time with her children fleeting.

"Going to work was not working," said Tawnya.

To make matters worse, the company she was working for soon folded, owing her weeks of back pay and without having delivered services to clients who had paid for them. At this point Tawnya did anything she could to provide for her children, from babysitting to mowing lawns, all the while thinking, *If I could just work from home I could be there for my kids and earn a living, too.* At her lowest point, she had to go to a food bank and get groceries to feed her children.

An opportunity lay in all of this misfortune and Tawnya was savvy enough to uncover it. In lieu of wages she was owed by her employer, she convinced her boss to give her his office equipment that she then used to set up a home office. She also convinced him to give her his old client list for whom she completed the work that had already been paid for without requiring additional compensation for her time. In doing so, she earned their trust and they continued to send more work her way.

Tawnya had just solved innumerable problems and helped many people. Her boss was relieved that he no longer owed her money, his clients were thrilled that they had their work completed without having to pay twice and she just set up her own company at no cost. She had now built herself a small business network as a virtual assistant.

"I didn't even know what a virtual assistant was back then," laughs Tawnya.

Six years later she found that the independent contract work she was doing for her clients left her isolated and without a support network. It was then she started up a unique social networking Web site called VAnetworking.com, where virtual assistants could post questions on issues such as software, grammar and billing. The majority of virtual assistants are work-at-home mothers. Instantly, a network began to grow and Tawnya was glad to be able to provide and gain support among her fellow colleagues.

There were still things Tawnya needed to learn in order to grow her business. She pursued certifications in Internet marketing and multimedia studies and went on to create a Virtual Assistant Start Up System which is now sold on the site. Those years where she juggled work and school admittedly took a toll on her family. One Mother's Day, her son gave her a greeting card with a note that put it all in perspective. "I love you Mom for making me happy," he wrote, "My Mother's Day wish for you is that you get all of your work done."

"For years, my kids thought all I did was work," said Tawnya. "They never came home and thought to look for me baking treats in the kitchen. They ran directly upstairs to look for me in my home office."

Nonetheless, Tawnya feels her children are at an advantage, because they witnessed their mother's hard work pay off with success.

"They know that you have to work for what you get in life and that things are not always given to you."

Today, VAnetworking.com is the largest virtual assistant social network in the world with more than 10,000 members, providing Tawnya and her family with more than $250,000 in income all from her home office. The site is free and offers a membership component with access to job postings as well as an at-home course on how to become a virtual assistant.

"You have to identify a problem and discover the solution to it," Tawnya recommends. "So many people are out of work today and, yes, the economy is going down. Yet virtual assistants are getting more work than ever because it is cheaper for a business to outsource work than pay full-time employees."

She also feels strongly about giving back and realized the reward in this from the feedback on her networking site.

"I get burned out like everybody else," said Tawnya. "Then someone sends me an e-mail saying 'Thank you— your kit helped me now be able to support my two kids and myself.' That's what it's all about." She keeps these messages in a "Feel Good" folder on her computer.

Being a Good Samaritan has rewarded Tawnya on many occasions. Once she stopped to help a woman with a flat tire who ended up being a reporter. That reporter ran a news story on the incident, bringing Tawnya's business great publicity.

"You never know who you might meet in the grocery store or anywhere."

Being able to identify which of her client's problems need to be solved by her versus which can be outsourced has been an important part of Tawnya's daily work strategy. She outsources more than 300 hours of work a month, something she wishes she would have seen the value in earlier. Housework and other domestic chores she outsources as well to someone else who is solving a problem for her so that she can be productive in her own business.

Remember: Volunteer and you will meet and network with new people who might help you on your road to success.

Exercise #12
From Rule No. 12: Help Yourself by Helping Others First

How to Find the Right Place to Give Back

This list may take a few days to create. Write a few things down just before you go to bed at night -- when your mind is clear. Think of things you loved to do as a child. Consider sports, hobbies, activities, interests, talents, passions.

Things I Love to Do	Ways I Do It Well	Organizations That Can Benefit from These Attributes

Chapter Thirteen

Rule No. 13

Don't Pray for What You Want, Pray for What You Have

A lot of people in many countries grow up dreaming big—the big house, the fancy car and the happily ever after. In many popular fairy tales you have read in your childhood, the plotline goes something along these lines: Girl is alone. Girl meets prince. Prince is dashing and rich. Prince sweeps girl off her feet and they ride off into the sunset to live in a castle. It is very romantic and can be seductive. So does this mean that if you don't meet a prince or don't become a prince that there may not be a sunset, castle and happily ever after for you? Of course not. But often people allow what constitutes happiness to be measured by what they can see: a handsome successful man, a beautiful woman, achieving children, a gorgeous home. When you realize that you are not in the picture, the dream shatters. Should happiness be measured? Or should it be felt?

The National Institute of Mental Health reports that major depressive disorder is the leading cause of disability in the United States for ages fifteen to forty-four. Major depressive disorder affects approximately 14.8 million American adults, or about 6.7 percent of the U.S. population age eighteen and older, and many more worldwide, in a given year. While major depressive disorder can develop at any age, the median age at onset is 32.5. The disorder is more prevalent in women than in men.

By the age of 32.5, most people have pretty much figured out if they are "in" or "out" of the Norman Rockwell portrait. Or maybe they are living a Norman Rockwell portrait that is as one-dimensional as any piece of art. Yet who determined that this version of happiness is what happiness truly is? We did.

It's evident that in today's culture we glamorize material objects. The goal of many lead characters in popular television game shows is to prevail at the sake of their competition so that they can win big money. We don't applaud people and highlight them for their teamwork and ability to motivate others. We vote people out of a competition and highlight their humiliation as they walk away. We criticize their performances and make fun of them for entertainment purposes.

Few professional athletes achieve for the love of their games as they did during the years when their salaries were less than the average annual income. Many wait to become free agents and, after years of playing on the same team, walk away for bigger money. I grew up watching the Pittsburgh Steelers. Money did not seem to motivate any of the 1970s Steelers. Today, the culture is much different and there is a lot of room for disappointment.

So how do you find peace in a world where fortune, fame and youth rule? After observing many truly peaceful people as well as many angry ones I have come to believe that the difference boils down to one thing—faith. Faith is based on the interpretation of the intangibles (feelings, emotions, etc.) instead of the physical tangibles (big house, fancy car). An expression of faith is prayer. In prayer we recognize the presence of God. It is the place where pride is abandoned, hope is lifted and, in appropriate circumstances, an appeal is made. Prayer is the place of admitting our vulnerability, of adopting humility and claiming dependence upon God. Faith is the absence of fear, while prayer is our reminder that we need not be afraid.

So if faith is about feelings and emotions, are you praying for the right thing? Are your prayers asking for something that is measured or intangible? Are you praying that you'll get the job with the higher salary? Or, are you praying to find a career that will make you feel happy to be at work every day? Are you praying that your business will become publicly traded within two years? Or are you praying that your idea will fill a need in society that people will want in order to make their lives easier? Are you praying for your health ailment to disappear? Or are you praying for the peace of mind to appreciate the wonderful things in your life today?

There were years that my life was filled with fear. When I became the primary and often sole provider for my children, I truly feared that I would not be able to provide food, shelter and necessities let alone college educations for them. It saddened me to think that I would not be able to give them a stable family life. I believed that the financial aspects of a family were what provided security. I wasted so much time praying to win in divorce proceedings that I really lost sight of the fact that what I was truly losing was my faith in myself and the trust that I've established in a higher power, such as God.

Having been through a divorce that lasted seven years, I honestly can say that the proceedings were the biggest waste of energy of my life. I recommend mediation in a divorce process. The only ones who win otherwise are the lawyers.

If I had it to do all over again I would have given away all of the tangibles right away—our house in an affluent suburb that was nearly paid off, automobiles, money and more—and simply walked away with what are truly of value: peace, integrity and faith. That is all you need to succeed. I know this, because I had the opportunity to learn it. My children, peace, integrity and faith are all that I left my marriage with and are the only things that are important in life. They are what delivered me to where I am today.

Unfortunately, divorce is set up to be divisive. Two people who, at one time, loved each other are full of hurt. They hire attorneys to defend their positions, confusing this work for hire with loyalty. The person in the marriage who controls the money ultimately controls the divorce. And the system, although well-thought-out and fairly productive, is not designed to give anyone a conscience.

Attorneys are business people who, like all effective business people, work for themselves—not you. The good ones try to work things out in the best interest of the children. The less moral see the children as casualties of war.

Faith is a source of strength from which you can regain your energy. When you don't trust it, fear slithers in, carrying on its back a magnification of evil. Things begin to seem much worse than they are. You get caught in a downward spiral of exaggerations that are not reality. If you allow evil to have power in your life, it will prevail in bringing you down. Even the intangibles become compromised—your ability to love, care, have faith. Only you control your peace, your integrity and your faith. Nothing and nobody can take that away. Faith is a major source of strength when you feel weak. It opens the latch and sets you free from the burden of fear.

Today, I feel all the things I worried about regarding my children were exaggerations of my own self-doubt. Of course, I was fully capable of taking care of and providing for my children. All they wanted to feel was that I loved them. That is not to say there weren't difficult times. We were rarely able to afford eating out at a restaurant and never did we order anything but water to drink. Once I stood in line at the grocery store with a child on each hip grateful that I had food stamps to purchase their food. I was very thankful that our family doctor continued to care for us when all we had was medical assistance to pay him. Gentle words of professionals assured me that the children would receive free school lunch without their friends knowing and that we could get assistance with our gas bill. The bank teller who recognized me from church cashed my welfare check without a hint of scrutiny. These are people who have earned my gratitude.

Yes, my faith was challenged. One day I returned from the town pool with my kids in the car to find a Sheriff's Sale notice taped to the front door of the home we had lived in for more than ten years and that was nearly paid off. The battles of a malevolent divorce had resulted in very poor judgments that were wearing on the fiber of our family. It was then that I decided that outside influences would no longer compromise anything that was dear to our family. I crumbled up the notice and immediately threw it away. As I tossed that preprinted notice into the garbage can, I felt as if I was shedding the skin of an old life that had done nothing but stifle what was crucial to my happiness. And it wasn't a house, a car, a country club membership or anything I could collect. My values are multidimensional and much richer. Among them was the joy one of my daughters and I felt together preparing her campaign slogans and T-shirts when she ran for student council in fourth grade, even though she didn't win. It was the delight in having girls from my Girl Scout Troop spot me in the community and run across the street to give me a big hug. It was the awe I felt when another daughter made me a Christmas ornament with her photo inside. It was the smiles my son gave me as a newborn bouncing in his Sassy Seat. And finally, it was the hug my oldest daughter and I shared when she gave me a handmade ceramic box for Mother's Day, on the inside of which she had painted "Mom, All you need is love."

My goal in this book has been to share the strategies that helped me so that others may shed fears and pursue their passions on journeys to greater peace and success. I found I needed nothing but the love in my own heart to provide a stable family life for my children and find success in my career. We did indeed purchase a wonderful home that we love. My children did indeed go on to college and are creating their own autonomous destinies in ways I never dreamed that will far surpass my own successes and I couldn't be more proud.

If you believe in a divine faith as I do, pray for what brings you the most peace. Have faith that you will get there. What do you really want to win? Peace of mind? The ability to love and be loved? Strength to create your own destiny? You have these things already.

Rule Break: Don't see prayer as your chance to put in your order for a better life. See it as an opportunity to be thankful for the good things already in your life.

Ways to Give Thanks:

1. Read a story of thanks. Set aside a few moments to sit down and read an uplifting short story. You can read it alone or together with your family. There are plenty of these stories in magazines and on the Internet. Search the Web under "ways to give thanks."
2. Write a prayer of thanks.
3. Share an experience from your past when you felt thankful. If there isn't anyone to share it with, write the experience down for later reflection.
4. Invite a widow, widower, single person or a person who is lonely to share a family meal or for coffee.
5. Prepare a meal to give to a needy family or a soup kitchen or a meal for a needy program.
6. Adopt a poor family for a holiday and provide their meal groceries in advance.
7. Make a blessing basket for your family. Place a pretty fall basket containing a pencil and pad of paper in an easy-to-reach location. Throughout the month, encourage family members to jot down things for which they are thankful. These can be jotted on cut-out leaves and placed on a paper "Thankful Tree" mounted to a wall or mirror.
8. Write a letter to someone in your life whom you never appropriately thanked. It could be to a family member, mentor or friend. Deliver it in person.
9. Keep a "Gratitude Journal" whereby you list things each day for which you are thankful. On the days when you feel depressed or if fear is threatening your peace, read the journal for a pick-me-up.
10. Look hard at the people who bring you the most pain or frustration and see what it is about them for which you are grateful. Do they teach you patience? It may be hard, but if you search the answer it will bring you great reward.

Lisa's Story

Lisa Stancati grew up in the late 1970s and early 1980s in Queens, New York, where both she and her father were huge baseball and football fans. When it came time for college, as much as Lisa loved the New York Mets and the Dallas Cowboys, she knew that opportunities for women in the sports arena were limited and followed her mother's more practical advice of pursuing a college degree in Legal Assistance. While working full time for a law firm, she entered law school at night and continued with that firm as a lawyer after she passed the bar examination. Later she moved to several other law firms, building her expertise in litigation and eventually securities law. Within days of switching to securities, Lisa was beginning to realize that all she had worked for was not working out.

"At that time I was so miserable doing what I was doing, I used to cry at night," said Lisa, who could not envision herself working in that specialty the rest of her life. Lisa was being considered to be made a partner in the firm at one point, if it were not for one thing.

"I used to look around the firm and I couldn't find one happy partner," said Lisa. "They all seemed miserable to me." Still, she and her colleagues fretted over whether or not they'd make partner, because after all, that is what every young lawyer wanted. Wasn't it?

Not for Lisa. "I knew it was time for me to take control of my own destiny and start moving in a different direction."

That summer, Lisa decided to take a break from the courtrooms of New York City to escort her ten-year-old nephew, Marty, to Jay Novacek Football Camp in Commerce, Texas. Jay had played tight-end for her favorite team—the Dallas Cowboys. While most of the parents dropped their kids off at the dorms of Texas A&M and left, Lisa checked into a local bed-and-breakfast, bought a lawn chair at a local store and sat on the field every day to watch Marty train.

"There wasn't a female within a mile-and-a-half," laughs Lisa, who rarely had to pay for a meal that week. On the flight home, she began to realize from her conversations in Texas that she really did know a lot about sports and remembers saying to herself, "Gee, I always loved sports. That's what I can do with my career." As soon as Lisa returned home, she signed up and began taking evening courses in sports marketing at New York University. She had to hide her desire to work in the sports field from her law partners who believed all associates should consider themselves lucky to be doing what they were doing.

A year and a half after earning her certificate in sports marketing, Lisa had stepped up her efforts to network and find a job in the sports industry. She was so dedicated to do whatever it took to break into sports, she even interviewed for a secretarial position with a sports executive at a national newspaper. She was willing to walk away from her six-digit salary, accept a pay cut and move back home to break into the industry. The sports executive laughed at her.

Still, Lisa remained even more committed to changing fields. Her network of friends started to bring opportunities her way.

"I told myself that if I have to eat peanut butter and jelly sandwiches until further notice, that's what I'll do," she said.

One of Lisa's colleagues opened the door for her to leave the high-powered salary and courtroom drama behind to become the executive director of the Women's Professional Billiards Association.

"Is that what you went to law school for?" her mother cried, echoed by the sentiments of her friends. "Are you nuts? Pool?" Nevertheless, Lisa was elated and energized.

"I told everyone 'trust me'," she said. "I knew I had to take a leap of faith in order to break into sports and sometimes you have to go backward in order to go forward again." An evolution began as she started to trust in the good things that were coming her way.

Yet all was not a panacea. Fifteen months later, the business relocated its offices to North Carolina and, in her thirties, Lisa was laid off with mounting bills and an expensive New York City apartment.

"All I heard was 'I told you so,'" said Lisa, who went back to pounding the pavement with an uncompromising resolve to find a new opportunity in sports. Eventually she was offered to take a temporary position as a paralegal with the National Hockey League.

"I took that job kicking and screaming, because it was a temporary gig and I wanted a full-time job, plus I was an attorney, so why should I accept a paralegal position?" she remembers. The recruiter advised her to just get in the door and prove herself. And prove herself she did: Lisa was eventually hired full-time as a lawyer in the NHL.

In her three years with the NHL, Lisa learned the licensing business as well as intellectual property law—skills she would never have learned working only in securities and litigation. But it was 2004 and the NHL was headed for a lockout. The league announced massive layoffs and Lisa's job was one of the casualties.

"I was forty, dateless and now jobless," said Lisa. "It doesn't get more depressing for a woman."

By this time, however, Lisa was seasoned at change. "It was becoming clearer to me that everything happens for a reason and if you just pay attention to—and heed—the messages the universe sends, bigger and better beginnings and opportunities abound," she said. "I said to myself, *Lisa, you don't really like this place anyway so what's so bad about leaving it?*" While her fellow terminated associates were crying and upset the night the NHL gave notice of the layoffs, Lisa ordered champagne and celebrated.

"I can't really explain it," she said. "I felt the universe was going to take care of me."

On Lisa's last day at the NHL when all her boxes were packed and she was about to exit the building for the last time, ESPN called her for an interview. Thereafter through a series of unrelated events, connections and what she calls "divine intervention", Lisa was offered a job in ESPN's Legal Department. Currently, Lisa is Assistant General Counsel at ESPN in their New York City office.

"I think you earn good karma," said Lisa. "I firmly believe that if you are willing to help yourself—to do your part—the universe will reward you. No matter what you want in life, life WILL throw you curve balls and challenges. Welcome them. They test your resolve and make you grow."

Lisa feels she has finally hit her stride and is looking for ways to give back. She volunteers her time mentoring students. Her goal is to start a non-profit organization to help coach young people on how to take responsibility, to make choices that are right for them and plan and achieve fulfilling careers.

"Follow your passion," she recommends. "Deal with the punches and setbacks. Perseverance and true passion will get you through that."

Remember: Decide what your goals are in life and envision yourself succeeding in gaining them.

Exercise #13
From Rule No. 13: Don't Pray for What You Want,
Pray for What You Have

My Thankful Prayer List...

Below is a list of things that will help you define all the wonderful things for which you already have to give thanks. In the third column think specifically about each person/thing on your list and write down what emotion would bring them more peace. Remember—emotions are not seen. "I pray that Uncle Jimmy feels less afraid of losing his eyesight." Regarding your "interests," would it bring you peace to develop them? Improve them? "I pray that I continue to make time to appreciate my garden. I pray that I have patience when learning how to play the guitar." I bet you have a lot to be thankful for in your prayers.

I am thankful for...	Names and Specifics	My prayer for him/her/them/it is...
Me		
Family Members I Am Close To		
Family Members I Am Not Close To		
Close Friends		
Acquaintances Who Have Been Kind To Me		
Neighbors Who Could Use Special Prayers		
Work and Former Employment		
Work Colleagues		
People in My Church		
Professionals Who Guide Me		
Interests and Causes Important to Me		
Teachers		
Pets		
Others		

Chapter Fourteen

Rule No. 14

It's Not What You Say, It's How You Say It and What You Don't Say

Albert Mehrabian, a Professor Emeritus of Psychology at UCLA, studied to determine that there are basically three elements in any face-to-face communication: words, tone of voice and body language. People's feelings toward you are based on these three areas. What would you guess is the percentage that each of these elements carries? The study shows that whether or not someone likes or dislikes you has little to do with what you say but more how you say it. Words account for 7 percent of whether or not they like you, tone of voice accounts for 38 percent, and body language accounts for 55 percent. These statistics have been used over and over in speeches on communication techniques, because most people are surprised to learn that whether or not they will be liked or disliked is based 93 percent on their non-verbal communication.

Your eye contact, your facial expressions, the position of your head, arms and body—these are all indicators of what you think and who you are. If you cannot look someone in the eye, s/he wonders what it is you are hiding. A smile is the universal symbol of warmth and kindness. It is very hard to be mean, rude or disinterested in someone who is smiling at you. If your shoulders are squared and your mind is clear, you exude confidence. People will want to know who you are and what you have to say. Nod your head. It shows that you are attentive, in agreement and listening. Keep your hands in sight—out of your pockets, but not fidgeting with hair or jewelry.

Watch yourself in the mirror when you talk on the phone. Chances are your body language is contributing to the way you are being perceived. Sit up straighter in your chair. Smile more. Keep your arms and legs uncrossed so as to appear open to what you are hearing.

If someone says "I agree with you," and she is crossing her arms and pursing her lips from side to side with her head cocked back, do you believe her? Of course not. If you are waiting in a reception area for an interview or to meet with a potential customer, you know that his or her first impression will be what s/he sees when the interviewer opens the door to call you in to that person's office. You don't want to be slouched over fiddling with your shoelaces. You want to be sitting up straight reading over your materials or the daily newspaper—both of which give an indication of intelligence.

Eye contact should be maintained about 60 percent of the time. During the other times, look in the interviewer's general direction. Ask yourself, "Am I really interested in what she has to say?" If not, then find a way to be interested. Everyone has had at least one interesting experience, job, family situation or career move. There is always something to learn.

Always be on time. Anything less than on time is unprofessional. Do not be more than five minutes early for your appointments.

E-mail is a common form of communication and should not be used with any less formality than a handwritten note. Start every e-mail with a salutation line—Dear Sally. End every e-mail with a signature box that helps brand who you are—John Mark Cannon followed by your contact information and a tag line on how you solve problems—"Computer Problem Solver." Do not say anything in an e-mail that you would not say in person; watch your tone.

Your phone message will also say a lot about you. Your message should be in your voice and not a recording so that callers know they have the right number and have reached the right person. Make sure the message is polite, direct and businesslike. Return telephone calls promptly. Do not have music playing in the background or let children record the greeting.

A good handshake is vital in business. Make it strong and vital. It is appropriate to shake people's hands when you first meet them and again when you leave. Your handshake will tell a lot about who you are, so practice it to get it right.

Watch presidents and other politicians shake hands and you will see that while they are shaking hands their left arms extend to touch the greeted person's upper right arm. This is a warm gesture of power. Being able to read body language plays an important role in business and in life. Being able to read the social cues of others and being aware of your own posture exudes that you are intuitive, confident and competent. You do not want to leave the impression that you are distant and not sure of your merits, because you then become a risk to the organization instead of a problem solver.

Rule Break: If you are a woman, do not wait for a man to offer a handshake first. If you want to start speaking with someone, introduce yourself. Read their nametag, offer a handshake and identify who you are. Some examples are, "Hi, Deb Hartman. Please allow me to introduce myself. I am Mary Pat Wolff. And what is it that you do for Fisher Company?"

The Four "Yeses" of a Good Handshake:
1. *Are you standing?*
2. *Are you smiling?* He will like that you like him.
3. *Do you know what color her eyes are?* She will see your interest, integrity and honesty in good eye contact.
4. *Is your grip firm enough?* If not, your handshake may feel limp. Don't be overbearing or wimpy. Be functional and direct.

If you are introducing two people, make sure you know who the more "important" person is. Once you have determined this, remember to say that person's name first in the introduction. If your colleague is James Montana and the customer is Heather Simpson you would say, "Heather Simpson I would like to introduce you to my partner James Montana." Remember: The customer is always the most important person.

Smooth transitions in introductions will help to spark casual conversation. Follow an introduction with a comment about the person so the individual will know why he or she is being introduced. Your goal within the first few minutes of meeting or introducing a person is to make that person feel comfortable and to put him or her at ease so that the person will want to do business with you.

A business card is a useful tool to leave the person so that he or she may contact you in the future. Business cards are also a great way for you to organize your new friends and associates. You'll have all their contact information at your fingertips, or you may want to enter their contact information in a spreadsheet, your phone or other software so that you may keep track of follow-up contact.

You will never have a résumé in your pocket at all times, so why not have pertinent information on a business card? It is compact and portable. Many times, job seekers have the opportunity to give a business card to someone they just met casually. Rather than sending off hundreds of résumés to those you don't know, individual contacts met at a networking event could mean far more in securing the right job or opportunity. When meeting a person for the first time, talk with him or her first for a while before handing the person your card. You will want to decide whether or not he or she is someone you want to know further. Ask for the individual's card first. Prematurely handing out a business card gives the appearance of being too eager and may end up forming a negative relationship. A business card should complete a meeting with someone after connecting.

Having the ability to give your contact information to a person in an instant is what business cards provide. As far as your card design, black ink on white paper is recommended for those job-hunting. If you are in a creative industry you may want to use something more imaginative.

If you do not have your own business cards, they can be ordered online very inexpensively. Simply search online under "business cards" or "inexpensive business cards" and you will view a number of vendors and designs available.

Don't carry your business cards on you just during business functions. Have your business cards with you at all times, but do not keep them in your wallet or loosely in your purse. Purchase a special holder for your cards—one that is rigid to preserve their importance and condition. When you give out your card, you want the recipient to see how much you value what is on it. Put information on your business card that reminds people of how you can help them solve problems. If you take a business card from a person, make a point of studying it, commenting on it and clarifying information before putting it away.

Three Rules for Creating a Business Card That Makes the Phone Ring:
1. Always have your name with middle initial on the top of the card. Make sure any certifications or appropriate credentials with acronyms are listed after your name.

2. Underneath your name on separate lines list: your address, phone number, fax number (if you have one), e-mail address and Web site (if you host one). If you are working from home and do not yet have a dedicated business line, list your cell phone number and start answering your phone with your name: "Mary Lee Gannon, how may I help you?" Change your answering machine message to be professional: "This is Mary Lee Gannon. I am not able to take your call at the moment, but your call is important to me. Please leave you name and telephone number and I will return your call as soon as possible."

3. Leave room at the bottom of your card to list "solutions" to their business problems that you offer.

Sample Business Card:

Deborah G. Conway
123 Any Street
Anywhere, PA 15555
Phone: 555-555-5555
Email: dconway@anysite.com

Total service communications for businesses that don't need it full time.

Business writing, graphic design, newsletters, grant proposals, public and media relations, event planning and more.

Or

Diverse office management skills all are just a phone call away.

Front office management, bookkeeping, payroll, materials management, inventory and more.

Remember: Never go into a meeting unprepared.

Exercise #14
From Rule No. 14: It's Not What You Say,
It's How You Say It and What You Don't Say

Positive Body Language Checklist

Remember, these elements that you exhibit weigh in at these percentages when a person is determining if they like you or what you are saying: Words—7 percent, Tone of Voice—38 percent, Body Language—55 percent. Review this checklist after an interview or important meeting in order to determine if the other person was engaged in your discussion and interested. Then take the quiz again and rate yourself!

Quality	Body Language Message	Yes/No
Was the person Listening?	Leaning Forward, Ignoring distractions, Stillness, Head tiled slightly forward, Gaze fixed on you, Furrowed brow.	
Was the person Open?	Smiled, Arms open, Legs uncrossed, Prolonged eye contact, Gaze looking around and at you, clothing hanging loose.	
Was the person Bored?	Distracted—looking anywhere but at you, Repetitive actions such as tapping toes or a pencil, Tiredness, Slouching.	
Was the person Closed Off?	Arms crossed—one or both across the body or one on a desk, Hands tightly clasped, Legs crossed in a variety of positions or wrapped around a chair, Looking down or away, Heat tilted away and tucked down.	
Was the person Deceptive?	Anxiousness of being found out for something, Sweating, Minor twitches in facial muscles, Changes in voice tone and speed, Forced smiles, Jerky movements, Distracted with a hesitation in speech as they plan, Paying attention to unusual places, Fluctuation in body language.	
Was the person Defensive?	Hands clasped over vital organs, Knees together, Chin down, Arms held out, Any physical object may be held in front of the person as a barrier (from a pencil to a table), Straddling a reversed chair, Huddling into a smaller position, keeping their arms and legs in, Tensing up, Eyes flicking from side to side, Filtering answers through hands.	

Quality	Body Language Message	Yes/No
Was the person Angry?	Appears frustrated, Face and neck are red, Clenched fists.	
Was the person Fearful?	In a cold sweat, Pale, Drinking water, Complaining of a cough, No eye contact, Trembling lip, Stammering voice tremors, High-pitched voice, Elbows in, Defensive body language, Crossed arms and legs, Wringing hands.	
Was the person Sad?	Flat speech, Drooping body, Little eye contact.	
Was the person Embarrassed?	False smile, Downward and away gaze, Changing subject in conversation.	
Was the person Surprised?	Raised eyebrows, Widened eyes, Open mouth, Sudden backward movement.	
Was the person Happy?	Facial and body muscles relaxed, Smiles.	
When asked a question did the person Tell the Truth?	Eyes looked up and to the left. Uses contractions. "I didn't do it."	
When asked a question did the person Lie?	Eyes looked up and to the right. Will not use contractions. "I did not do it."	

Chapter Fifteen

Rule No. 15

Dress for the Job Above
the One You Want

What you wear has just become increasingly important. It may sound shallow, but how you choose to present yourself on the outside is a reflection of who you are on the inside. It is a precursor to how you will bring value to your prospective customers, clients or employer. Don't make your appearance a problem. You are trying to convince the person whom you meet that you can help him or her solve problems. Be a solution. Be neat. Exact. Finished. Make your appearance something they need not notice as a problem. Make it something that impresses them.

Observation is the best teaching tool. If you are trying to break into the corporate world or start a business with corporate clients, spend a lunch hour near a large corporate headquarters and notice how people dress. Are they wearing suits or business casual attire? What kind of coats do they wear? How do they wear their hair? Are they wearing a lot of jewelry? What style of briefcase are they carrying?

Can you tell the support staff from the executives? I bet you can. Even if you are vying for an entry-level position, dress like the executives, albeit within your budget. Why? Because the people hiring you will take note of how you view your own skill set. If you go on an interview, make note of how the interviewer dressed. Should you be dressing the same? Be true to who you are and adapt what you see to what you are comfortable with wearing.

Flip through a business or news magazine and note how those featured are dressed. Notice the models in business advertisements.

If you are working for a start-up or a younger company, notice what the employees in the office are wearing. Are they in conservative or leisure clothes? If you are breaking into a creative field, do people dress in free spirited styles? Do not be extreme but be comfortable bringing your own personal style to your appearance. No matter what the employees are wearing in the office, it is best to dress conservatively for the interview.

Shoes: Newer stylishly understated shoes are vital. People naturally look down when they are walking. It is how they make sure they do not trip. Whatever shoes you wear, make sure they look new and are not outdated. Worn-out shoes are a sign of worn-out enthusiasm and an unkempt life. If you are a woman breaking into the corporate world, shoes should not have open toes and always wear panty hose at an interview. Handbags should look new as well and not be oversized. Both shoes and handbags should be conservative and traditional.

Accessories: Keep them at a minimum. If you wear earrings, make sure they are not more than one inch long. Ask yourself whether you should wear less jewelry or not. If you wear earrings, do you also need a necklace? Wear a watch and only wear one ring per hand.

Hair: Hair should be styled and not loose flying. If your hair is long, pull it back from your face. You have nothing to hide. For men, facial hair should be groomed often.

Ladies: Do not wear plunging necklines. Choose a button-down shirt under your suit. Collars of shirts worn under suits should come to your clavicle or just below. Skirts should be knee length or longer. Make sure your nails are neat and trimmed. If you wear nail polish, it should be clear, pale pink or some other natural color.

Gentlemen: Wear button-down shirts and a tie with your suits.

If you need a new work wardrobe, where should you buy it? Certainly department stores usually carry very appropriate business wear. I'd invest in a classy dark suit as opposed to several casual outfits. Consignment shops and thrift shops often have very nice suit jackets as well, which are not worn or tattered. People often grow tired of suits or put on weight before they wear them out. Take time to go through the racks of clothes at thrift shops as the clothes are generally not typically sorted by size. Be careful that the styles are not outdated.

Before you start a new job, check with the Human Resources office (if the business has one) as to the dress code policy and follow it exactly. Otherwise, observation is key. Often businesses will have a "business casual" dress code or a business casual day once a week. The parameters of business casual vary from company to company, so make sure you check. Generally business casual means that suits are not required. Men can wear khaki pants and collared shirts without ties. Women can wear slacks and knit tops. No jeans. I still recommend attending an interview or a potential customer meeting in a business suit. You are not an employee; you do not have their business yet.

Business casual is the dress code that you will find most common-place in offices today. The interpretation of this term is the broadest and should be confirmed with your Human Resources department. Clothing should be conservative. Button-down shirts, trousers, blouses, sport coats and skirts are suitable. Shoes need not be polished leather. Leather loafers or similar styles are acceptable. Avoid sneakers and sandals.

As a single parent of four children having an executive level position I do not have a lot of time to shop, accessorize or update my wardrobe for every season. I have always been a devotee of classic clothes. Classic clothes rarely go out of style and hold their value long after their purchase. I'd rather purchase a very good suit jacket than three trendy sweaters. No matter whom you are meeting with or selling to, traditional clothing will always be appropriate. A pair of very good black or brown pants will last much longer than six pairs of pants with trendy leg widths and belt loops.

Early on, I decided to dress for work in a suit jacket. Why? Because I am a professional and that is what executives in my industry wear. If your office has a different dress code and no human resource department, look at what the senior team wears to work. You may not be able to afford the same designer lines that they wear, but if they are wearing suits, you can wear one, too. If they dress casually but tastefully, you can, too. Dial down the sex appeal. Skinny heels are only for lower-heeled shoes. Observe. It is an easy thing to do.

When you wear more powerful looking business attire, switching from "relaxed mode" to "professional mode," it changes your mind-set. This positive change begins to affect your attitude and becomes reflected in your body language and behavior (e.g. better posture, firmer handshake, maintaining eye contact, sticking to business, etc.), thus giving you greater visual power.

For me, accessories have always had a strong place in my wardrobe. Accessories allow you to incorporate trends at affordable prices. If you are a woman, suits take on an entirely different look with a chic scarf. Jewelry can give your neckline an entirely different appearance. A belt can dress up a very plain pair of pants. Piercings anywhere besides women's ears (one or two per ear) must be removed. Tattoos must not be visible.

A designer purse makes a strong statement for a woman, but only if your shoes are newer and tasteful. The right purse and shoes can often make a fashion statement far easier than your clothes and you can wear them more then once every few weeks. I think a good wallet (not necessarily designer) and a sleek business card holder are essentials as well. No faux leather in accessories—including the briefcase.

In a recent *Wall Street Journal* poll, 53 percent of CEOs reported that they preferred blue, dark blue or navy blue suits and 39 percent chose gray, charcoal or dark gray. For both men and women, dark suits convey authority, conservatism and confidence. The preferred shirt color was white with blue as second choice.

For men in more formally dressed places of employment, the tie is the accessory that makes a statement—100 percent silk is best. Make sure the geometric patterns are miniscule. CEOs report that dark ties are favored.

Save the red power tie for an important meeting.

Bookstores and checkout lines are perfect places to skim through fashion magazines for the latest trends. But in terms of your wardrobe for the office, seek classic looks with perhaps a trendy accessory for a professional appearance.

Rule Break: Men often take their suit jackets off at work. If you are a woman just breaking into a new environment, I say do not. Chances are you do not have on a button-down shirt with a tie under your suit. The top you have on under your jacket will look less professional than your male counterparts' attire.

The Mirror Check Before You Leave the House
Women and Men:
* *Purchase an inexpensive full-length mirror and place it across from your dresser mirror so that you can see yourself from the back in the mirrored reflection.* Do not leave for work before doing a 360-degree check of your appearance. Are your pants wrinkled? Iron them. Is there lint on your jacket? Use a lint roller. Are there panty lines?

Women:
* *Is your hair neat and styled?* From behind, too?

❋ *Are you wearing the appropriate accessories?* Two or three pieces of jewelry are plenty. Does your handbag match your shoes? Are they leather? Do they look new? Do your shoes match the color of your pants or skirt or do they stand out like bricks on your feet? Socks should match your shoes. Panty hose should as well unless they are neutral.

❋ *Does your makeup blend neatly into your skin or are there clumps of color around your cheeks, eyes and/or lips?* Go for the clean look. The only real color that is noticeable on your face should be in your lipstick. And even there subtle is better.

❋ *Are your nails neat and your hands smooth?* Loud-colored nail polish is not professional. Neither is chipped nail polish. People will be looking at your hands all day—as you hand them reports, shake hands, answer the telephone. Make sure you have hand cream and a nail file in your desk and on your dresser at home. If you are not able to keep your nails painted, just keep them filed and at a reasonable length. Or try a clear or pale pink polish which does not show as much when it starts to chip. (The nail file at work is ONLY for broken nails.)

Men:
❋ *Is your haircut neat and recent?*
❋ *Are you well-groomed and shaved?*
❋ *Are your suit and clothing appropriate?*

Women and Men:
❋ *If your company has a lapel pin, do you have it on every day?* This is a sign of your dedication to the mission of the company.

Remember: Nothing says success better than someone who is well-dressed.

Exercise #15
From Rule No. 15: Dress for the Job Above the One You Want

Top Tier Gear

Below is a list of the quintessential dress requirements for professionals or for an interview. Check off these items as you know that you have them prepared. You only have a few seconds to make a first impression so make sure you are comfortable, clean, neat and professional. And smile!

Item	Recommended Top Tier Gear
Suit:	A conservative, well-fitted, two-piece dark blue or a dark gray business suit. For women the skirt should be knee length or longer.
Shirt:	A white, long-sleeved tailored dress shirt that is neatly pressed.
Briefcase:	Bring a leather briefcase with a notepad and a pen for taking notes.
Hair:	Make sure that your hair is well-groomed. Short or pulled back hair fares best in interviews.
Nails:	Clean and trimmed. Women may use clear or neutral nail polish.
Piercings:	Visible body piercings other than earrings for women should be taken out.
Body & Breath:	Shower and brush your teeth. No strong cologne. Eat a breath mint ahead of time.
	Accessories for Women
Shoes:	Wear leather closed-toe conservative shoes that match your suit. No narrow heels.
Jewelry:	Two to three pieces of jewelry are best. One of those should be a watch. Only one or two earrings should be worn in each ear and they should not exceed one inch in length.
Hosiery:	Pantyhose are a must and should be a neutral color.
Handbag:	Handbag should be a conservative leather bag—designer if possible. No imitations.
	Accessories for Men
Tie:	Go for a dark plain colored non-distracting tie made of 100 percent pure silk. A classic silver tie bar will ensure that your tie is held in place during the interview.
Shoes:	Clean and polished conservative leather dress shoes, black lace-ups if possible.
Socks:	Socks should be dark, black if possible.
Belt:	The belt should match the color of your shoes, black if possible.
Beard:	A beard needs to be shaved off. Mustaches are a possible negative, but if you must, make sure it is neat and trimmed.
Jewelry:	Wedding or college rings are generally acceptable but nothing else.

Chapter Sixteen

Rule No. 16

Create a Simple Portfolio
with a Binder and Sheet Protectors

If you can show a potential employer or client work that you have done, it will go a long way to instill confidence and remove any risk they may have in hiring you. A portfolio is a collection of the best examples of your work. No matter what kind of work you do, showcase it in your portfolio. Go to your local office supply or discount store and purchase a two-inch binder and a box of sheet protectors. Sheet protectors are clear plastic sleeves that are three hole punched to hold items you want to display in the binder. Now, you may think that you have not done any work that you can put in your "portfolio." Think again.

If you have written anything for any sort of publication and are marketing your writing skills, use it. This could be a church newsletter, a letter to the editor, etc. If you have worked on a fundraiser as a volunteer include the fliers, invitations, any other planning materials and the final financial report. Include photographs of anything you worked on such as a 5K run or a large party that you planned. Do not include photos of your family.

Always put samples of key things you have worked on or accomplished in your portfolio. The portfolio will also serve as a reference for future planning and interviews.

The most important thing you will put in your portfolio are letters of reference from previous employers, colleagues and friends. Any time you resign from a position or your boss moves to another position, ask your boss for a general letter of recommendation addressed: To Whom It May Concern. Make it easy for your boss to write such a letter by giving him or her bullet points that highlight your key accomplishments. I have many of these in the front of my portfolio.

When I first started writing professionally, I saved clippings of my articles from the newspapers and magazines for which I wrote. I made sure the clips were dated and had the title of the publication on each. Over time, the clips were yellowing so I began copying them and putting them in the described portfolio. I kept them in chronological order. This helped me find specific clips when I needed them. Then I took a position in the corporate world and for many years wrote only in connection with my work. When I decided to try to sell this manuscript to a publisher, I needed to demonstrate my writing background. My clips portfolio came in handy. Had I not organized my writing years before, I would not have been able to reference it. I also have a professional portfolio for my corporate work; I still reference these portfolios.

Rule Break: Do not discard work that you have done in the recent past, because you think it will not be of value later. Chronicle everything that you are doing. Nothing is insignificant. If you have coached a girls' basketball team, include the roster of players and plans you created for plays. Maybe someone who is mentoring you could use some help coaching his daughter's or her son's team. As the work you do increases in intensity, you will need fewer of these things, because your portfolio will be full of your successes in career-oriented objectives.

Portfolio Samples: (Show How You Have SOLVED PROBLEMS!)
Manager: Include hard copy examples that demonstrate how you did so—scheduling sheets, budget spreadsheets, process descriptions, job descriptions that you wrote and meeting action plans.

Chef: Include menus, newspaper clippings of your reviews, photographs of your creations from an event, written recipes, certifications, inspection reports and letters of reference from restaurant owners.

Bookkeeper: Include a detailed list of the software systems you have used, copies of reports you have prepared, overall budget spreadsheets.

General Contractor: Include photos of the projects you have worked on during different phases of the projects as well as close-up photos of your construction techniques, records that illustrate your ability to meet deadlines, safety results and training certificates.

Event Planner: Make sure to include samples of the event budgets, photos of various aspects of the events, timelines, invitations and final reports.

Remember: An organized portfolio is key.

Exercise #16
From Rule No. 16: Create a Simple Portfolio with a Binder and Sheet Protectors

What to Put in Your Portfolio

A collection of real examples of your work shows what you can do and makes you stand out in an interview or when you are selling your service or product to potential clients. Your portfolio is as simple as a binder with sheet protectors. Build a case for your strengths inside.

1. Résumé: Put your résumé on the first page. Make sure that your résumé stresses your measurable accomplishments. Have extra copies behind it.

2. Letters of Reference: Second and most important in your portfolio should be letters of reference. The more you have, the better. Anyone with whom you have worked can be asked to write a letter of reference or recommendation. The higher placed this person is professionally, the better it will be for you. A friend, colleague, pastor or former employer could write you a letter. Make sure the author of the letter is someone who knows you well and ask him or her to list their title after their signature. If it is a friend whom you worked with on a committee, make sure she lists her title on that committee and the name of the organization it served: Mary Thompson, Chairman of the PTA, St. Anselm School. Always have two to three letters of reference. Always ask for a letter of reference from every place you have worked when you resign. Always ask for a letter of reference from your boss if he or she leaves before you do. These are the most valuable parts of your portfolio.

3. Awards and Recognitions: This section holds copies of any awards that you have received in chronological order.

4. Budgets: Include samples of any budgets that you have managed in your professional life. If you have not worked professionally for a while, did you have a budget for the team you coached? The committee you chaired? The fundraiser you worked on? Do you manage a household budget? If you can demonstrate that you know how to manage money, you will demonstrate value.

5. Creative: This section holds samples of anything you have worked on or designed—fliers, invitations, newsletters, etc.

6. Writing: Here you want to include copies of anything you have written for semi-professional purposes—newsletter articles, an overview of a situation or a report for a meeting.

7. Media: Find copies of clips from the newspaper that featured you, a project on which you worked or lead the charge.

8. Photographs: Include photos of events you worked on and photos of any other achievements.

Chapter Seventeen

Rule No. 17

Read the Newspaper Every Day—
Or Get Current, World and Local News
How You Like It

Some may say that this is an important rule to me, because I used to write for newspapers. That may be true. But the reason I believe you should read the newspaper daily is not because I am a fan of print media. I have found that I am able to keep up with any conversation at a business lunch, interview, sales meeting, customer meeting and any situation by simply reading a metropolitan newspaper every day. Others find television and Internet news provides this information as well. I enjoy television news, especially the national evening news.

I understand that the newspaper business is a dying industry, because they heavily rely on income from classified advertising, which has since migrated to Internet-based venues such as Craig's List for household items and Monster.com for employment. But within a short amount of time in the morning, I can get a recap of yesterday's news and the evening news highlights at a time that is convenient to me by reading the morning paper. And an added bonus is that I love *The Family Circus, Dennis the Menace* and *Marmaduke* cartoons in the funny pages.

A newspaper offers you the opportunity to scan at a glance what might interest you. It affords you the luxury of reading the entire story or just the first few paragraphs—whatever time permits. You can scan a page and see what interests you without having to listen to or read about things that are not of interest to you.

My suggestion is to at least read the lead, or first few paragraphs, of every story on the front pages of each section. I find that in ten to fifteen minutes I can gain enough information from the newspaper that I am not left out in the dark of a conversation if someone brings up a current event. On an interview or first meeting, don't overemphasize a current issue by bringing up the news. Only reference the news if it is relevant to the conversation, if it seems natural to do so or if asked about it.

Who are your local politicians? What important decisions do they influence that affect you, the people of your town or the business in which you are seeking work? What issues are your school board members voting on that affect your taxes? Has crime risen or declined in your community and how does that affect local businesses? All of the answers to these questions are in your city newspaper.

It is good to know who won the game last night and whom your home team played. Sports in general may not interest you, but something about it may be interesting either to you or your interviewer. Is the cost of a new stadium for your town going to impact taxes? Is the star player going to sign his contract, because if he does not, attendance may drop, affecting restaurant business downtown?

If you know what is currently occurring in your town and the world, it shows that you are intelligent enough to follow the news and understand its impact on the lives of those around you.

If you are on an interview or at a meeting and are asked to reference something in local politics or comment on a national issue that relates somehow to the company, knowledge about the subject will show that you are well-read and well-informed. As you begin to read the newspaper every day you will also find that news is interesting because it affects history. Journalists are generally polished writers and their writing is concise, easy to read and tight.

I especially like to read the business section of the paper. In this section I get a lot of leads for my work. I see who has been appointed as presidents of particular companies, what companies are doing well and which ones are not. Often I send notes of congratulations to my friends and colleagues, further building relationships based on what I read.

If access to a local daily paper is difficult, news from local newspapers can be found online. Scan the home pages of your local newspapers daily. You can set that as the page on which your computer opens whenever you access the Internet.

I also recommend reading your town's weekly business journal. Many who travel a lot for work do this to catch up on the week's business news. I do it, because the features generally give me insight on individuals and companies that the daily papers do not have space to cover. Every Friday, I clip out a story and send it along with a note of congratulations to someone I care about or add someone's name from the paper to my database of prospective contacts.

Expanding your network of friends and watching that continue to grow will broaden your possibilities for your future growth. It will keep you stimulated and disallow boredom and stagnation to creep into your ranks. There is much that can be learned and personal rewards can come from observing and cultivating relationships with others. My parents taught me this when I was very young and it has served me well.

How to Know the News:

1. Pick a specific time to read the newspaper or check news online and dedicate fifteen minutes to that every day. I find the best time to read the newspaper for me is before I leave for work. I get up, do some yoga and exercises, let my shih-tzu out and read the paper while she is outside. Set up your search engine home page with news links. Set up a time each day to watch your favorite television program or scan the newspaper Web site.

2. Leave the advertisement sections and click ads alone. Don't even open them.

3. Read the first four paragraphs of the lead story in the newspaper every day—this will be what most people will be talking about.

4. Read the lead paragraph of every story on the front page and the entire story of the ones that really interest you.

5. Read the first paragraph or two of each story on the front page of each section. It may seem a little overwhelming but keep doing it every day. You will see how the stories relate to each other and continue.

6. Ask yourself, "Isn't it interesting?"

Remember: Having a knowledge of current events is always a good way to break the ice during an initial meeting or conversation.

Exercise #17
From Rule No. 17: Read the Newspaper Every Day—
Or Get Current, World and Local News How You Like It

The "Am I Interesting" Quiz

Take this quiz to see if you are reaching out of your comfort zone to understand the current culture, current events and current trends around you.

	Yes	No
1. I have read a magazine in the last month that I have never read before.		
2. I have a page on an Internet social or professional networking Web site such as Facebook, Twitter, LinkedIn or Zoominfo.		
3. I read the newspaper, watch the evening news or check news online at least once a day.		
4. I have purchased a trendy article of clothing either new or at a secondhand shop in the past month.		
5. I have leafed through a fashion magazine at the checkout stand just to keep up on fashion trends within the past month.		
6. I have posted something new on my social or professional networking Web site of choice within the last three days.		
7. I have re-arranged my furniture or added a new accessory for a new home décor look in the past month.		
8. I have gone through my closet in the past two months and thrown out everything I haven't worn in a year.		
9. I've registered for a non-credit or credit class in the past month in something that I want to learn or have read a book about the topic.		
10. I attended a cultural production (play, musical, concert, poetry reading, etc.) within the past two months that I have not attended in the past.		
11. I've gone for a walk in the last week in an area I have not walked through before.		
12. I am exercising three times a week.		
13. I tried a new restaurant or recipe in the last week that I have not tried before.		
14. I invited a friend for coffee or to lunch within the past month whom I haven't seen in months.		
15. I invited a new friend for coffee or lunch with whom I have not done this in the past.		
16. I visited an exhibition, museum, festival or any other visual art display in the last month.		
17. I have changed my hairstyle—even if slightly within the past six months.		
18. I've purchased a trendy accessory such as a pair of shoes, purse, a tie or jewelry either new or gently used within the past two months.		

Now mark your calendar and take this quiz again in a month to see if you are more or less interesting. You make the choices in your life.

Chapter Eighteen

Rule No. 18

On the Interview Tell a Story and Ask More Questions Than the Interviewer Asks You

Whether you are starting your own business or going on an interview, the research you do ahead of time will make or break your first meeting with potential employers and customers. Potential clients and interviewers have a list of questions that they need answered in order to evaluate whether or not you will be able to help them better than any other candidate. The questions that you ask them are truly what will make you stand out.

Often potential employers will ask standard questions such as these: "Tell me about your work experience." "What salary are you making now?" "Tell me about your experience using (a specific software program)."

Open-ended questions are designed to draw out your personality and character traits. "Tell me a little about yourself" or "Tell me what isn't in the résumé" are common examples of this type of question. Answer these queries by showing examples of both your personal and professional accomplishments while including how your values led you to achieve these things.

Many consultants will advise you to keep your personal situation out of a job interview and I mostly agree. However, I have found that aspects of my personal and professional journey tell a compelling story. When I share a story, I keep all editorial comments about other people absent. If it concerns the aftermath of my divorce, I keep the details of how the children and I suffered out of it, because it is not relative to what we achieved. I simply focus on what challenges faced me and how I dealt with them. After all, prospective employers only care about how you will solve problems for them. Anecdotal examples of how you have already dealt with great challenges will erase the potential risk they might have in hiring you. Remember, in good stories, "showing" is much more effective than "telling." Don't tell them you are a hard worker, tenacious and dedicated. Convey that in your story. Allow the interviewer to draw that conclusion and feel the truth in it. It will mean much more.

For example, if an interviewer asks me to fill in the blanks of what is not on my résumé, the first thing I generally say is, "I am a single parent of four children, who, when my children were all under the age of seven, found that I had to recreate my life." At this point they usually sit up straight and look amazed. The silence in the room is deafening. I realize that with the way I set this up, the story better be good.

I go on to say, "I was in a difficult marriage (the details of which are not relevant to this meeting or anything else related to moving forward) and I became acutely aware as a stay-at-home mother with four children that I would need to become the primary source of income for my household. I reassessed my job skills and could see that I could not return to the career path of my college degree, because the pay in the allied health profession would not support five people. I analyzed what careers paid well and had a low barrier to entry. It seemed to me the career track that met these qualifications with unlimited opportunities was sales. So I mentored under a friend who was a sales professional. He graciously took the time to teach me the art of selling by allowing me to shadow him on sales calls. I could see that much of his success was rooted in his people skills, relationships and dedication to good customer service—not just price." (This narrative shows strategic thinking ability, that I value responsibility to my children and that I am a quick learner without having to "say" any of this.) The rule is, show don't tell.

From here I go on to explain that as a sales associate, my mentor recommended me to be the executive director of the trade association for this industry where I was able to increase trade show attendance by 150 percent in the first year (measurable results). I juggled that opportunity, freelance writing for several newspapers and magazines, being the public relations director of a public school district and other clients from my home office. Then I go on to say, "My school district client asked me to help them fundraise, so I taught myself how at the library and cold-called potential funders. I raised more than $500,000 for that district without being compensated and I never asked to be, as I appreciated the opportunity to learn this skill. They issued me a state award in gratitude. I should have issued them the award." You can see how the listener would postulate his or her own conclusions from this story without me telling them my values, work ethic or problem solving ability.

Make sure you have several personal success stories that you can share. Stories should average between thirty to ninety seconds. Practice telling these stories while you are driving. Make sure you have listened to yourself say them before you deliver them to another individual. Stories should revolve around these areas:

1. Made or saved money in a previous position.
2. Tragedy to triumph or turnaround story.
3. Functioned as part of a team, describing your contribution.
4. Leadership that drove a new direction for the company.
5. A professional failure that you overcame.
6. Career changing events.

Stories leave deeper impressions, because they are coupling visual images with problem solving techniques. Be sure to lace quantifiable results into the stories.

A prospective employer may ask you what your greatest work-related accomplishment was. Think of one that gave you great personal reward as well as gave the company great financial reward. Employers value accomplishments that reduce expenses, raise revenues and solve problems. I explained my greatest accomplishment as having led the charge that raised more than ten million dollars, twice the goal, to expand and open new programs that save lives while also leading my children to become thoughtful and productive members of society.

If asked, "What is your greatest strength?" always list three strengths and highlight your best one. Your best strength should show strategic thinking skills and an ability to juggle multiple projects. Your greatest strengths might be tenacity, dedication and innovation.

When asked about your weaknesses, be careful. Interviewers have heard the scripted answers of turning a positive into a weakness such as, "I take on too much work" or "I'm a perfectionist." I feel that you should be sincere. State a genuine weakness that you HAD and tell a story of how you overcame that weakness.

One of my weaknesses is that I used to expect others to work at the same pace and strategy as I did and sometimes expected that they knew what I expected without explanation. I do not micromanage, so what happened was that I ended up expecting certain outcomes without having explained my expectations or methods of achieving them. This weakness did not serve me well in management or as a parent. In order to overcome this, I studied management and behavior books and worked hard at stronger and more definitive communications methods by hosting staff meetings, creating metrics that are easy to follow for my staff and better communicating schedules and instructions to my children. Employers will appreciate an honest answer that demonstrates how you put together a successful plan to improve a certain weakness.

"Why do you want this position?" always is a question asked when the company is looking for loyalty and dedication. This is where the research you did on the company will pay off. Make sure you have answered this question in your own head before you go to the interview or you will look as if this is just one of a number of positions you would take. They want to know that this is the ONLY position you want, because you feel a stake in the mission of the company and will be more likely to work as if the goals of the company were your own.

If asked why you are the best person for the job, think about all of the "values" you "showed" during your stories and match those with the mission of the company. "I am committed to working for XYZ Company, because it has the same goals and vision that I do. XYZ Company is not only dedicated to its shareholders, but also to its employees. Your products improve quality of life. I would be inspired to sell them, because I believe they make a difference to the public. My past work ethic demonstrates that I would be as dedicated to this mission of XYZ, as I have been to everything else I have committed myself to."

Interviewing with a potential client will bring about questions that are somewhat similar to a job interview. "Can you give me a list of your clients?" "Are there examples of your work I can review?" "What do you charge?" Show them that you can handle challenges.

There are wonderful books in libraries and bookstores on how to shine during an interview. Review some of them, because they will help you feel more comfortable with what to expect. The purpose of this chapter is not to help you answer interview questions. There are many books that will advise you on how to do that. I want you to think in a broader direction. Know your own story and talk it out ahead of time. You can find advice online on how to practice for an interview as well. Simply search on "How to do well on an interview."

Before you go on an interview make sure you are comfortable with what to expect. Having answered the standard questions out loud in front of your mirror so that you will not appear to be on your first interview when you are there is crucial.

Visit the company's Web site and familiarize yourself with its mission. Use a search engine to locate its name and see if it has been in the news lately. Make sure you are able to convert what you have learned to appropriate conversation material for the interview. "I see that XYZ company recently was awarded Corporate Partner of the Year by ABC Hospital. You must value giving back to the community." "Did the debut of your (latest product) recently gain the results that you had planned?"

If you haven't worked in a while, be prepared to convert your volunteer commitments to results-oriented achievements. You didn't volunteer for your child's high school scholarship committee; you organized a review process to fairly evaluate candidates for college scholarships. You didn't volunteer for the PTA; you became proficient in Microsoft Office programs to organize membership records, track dues and send dues notices. You haven't been unemployed; you have been managing a family and home budget.

Again, the most important questions asked at an interview will be the ones that YOU ask. Good questions require research and the Internet will most likely give you information you need to know. Supplement this by conversations with people you know who work there and you will have inside insight. If you are going on an interview, search the company's Web site before you go. Be able to reference the things that are important to you as a potential employee. Do not ask about pay, hours or benefits until the interviewer offers you the job. Employers are looking for "Big Picture" thinkers. They are not looking for someone who wants to know what time they start and what time they can go home. They are looking for someone who can identify a better way to do something, suggest it with respect and implement the change without a lot of supervision. Remember—you are there to solve problems.

I always close an interview with the same question, "Is there any concern keeping me from being the lead candidate for this position?" They will be impressed with your candor and ability to address important issues. This is the point at which you have the opportunity to speak to any concerns that are in the way of your getting the job.

Rule Break: Yes, the interviewer is interviewing you. However, you are also interviewing the interviewer. You want the person to see that you are very interested in the company. Show your sincerity. The interviewer is a potential friend from whom you can gleam more insight than perusing the company's Web site.

Does Your Résumé Look Weathered?
Make sure your résumé reflects what employers today are seeking. Believe
that you have a lot to offer.
1.   Has your résumé grown to six or seven pages over time? Is your first
     job after high school graduation still listed? Are you still displaying the
     date you graduated from college? It is not required. Consolidate and
     update the material.
2.   Include only the most recent fifteen to twenty years of work history.
     The emphasis today is on capabilities, qualifications and achievements.
     Don't tell prospective employers that you can use various software
     programs. Give examples of how you helped the bottom line of a
     company in doing so.
3.   If your relevant accomplishments are three jobs back—don't list a
     chronology of your work history on your résumé. Prospective employ-
     ers may not read that far. Lead the professional section of your résumé
     with your list of accomplishments for each position.
4.   If you have been at home raising children for several years, call
     attention to your lifetime of experience—at home, in the community
     and at work. Think of accomplishments in terms of transferable skills:
     those in the areas of *communications, organizing information* and *fixing
     things.* You haven't simply been a stay-at-home mother. You have
     managed a budget that saved for family vacations, college tuition funds
     and retirement. Not to mention, you organized a fundraiser at your
     children's school that raised $11,000 for new computers. You wired all
     the electronics in your home including computers, printers and scan-
     ners, as well as set up all the software programs for such.
5.   Focus on your positive attitude. Potential employers want to know that
     you have a deep openness to learning new things. They want people
     who are willing to learn, adapt and are stable, who are looking for the
     next job before starting this one. Communicate these strengths in your
     résumé. You can do it.

Remember: Review your Life Balance chart from exercise 5.

Exercise #18
From Rule No.18: On the Interview Tell a Story and Ask More Questions Than the Interviewer Asks You

Ten Questions for You to Ask the Interviewer that Scream "I Get the Big Picture!"

Fill out this questionnaire after every interview to evaluate yourself and the prospective company.

1. How long does the average employee stay with your company? (You hope that employees are staying with a company for at least three to five years. Depending on the field it can be longer. Healthcare tends to keep its workers longer. Those working for the government stay the longest. If the company has a high turnover rate, this may not be the place for you.)

2. Could you describe the type of employee who fits well within your organization?

3. How important does upper management consider the function of this department/position?

4. In my research I have learned what your company values are. What is the company's management style?

5. Have key people left the company? Why? Where did they go?

6. What is the biggest challenge your company has right now? (This will give you the company's "problem" that you want to help solve. Offer ways that you can contribute to solving that problem. "So you need people who can work on their own without direction.")

7. What is the organization's plan for the next five years?

8. What are the company's strengths and weaknesses compared to its competition?

9. What's the most important thing I can do to help within my first ninety days?

10. Do you have any concerns that I need to clear up in order to be the top candidate? (This is where they will have the opportunity to state any concerns they may have about you such as not having been employed in a while.)

Chapter Nineteen

Rule No. 19

Expect Everything—
Nothing is Gravy

Remember when you were a small child and you wanted that one special present for your birthday or a holiday? You wanted it so badly that you used to dream about it. You used to lie in the grass in your backyard and see it in the cloud formations. You may have even drawn pictures of it. You envisioned yourself using it. You probably talked to your friends about it. Surely you told your parents about it and maybe even your grandparents. Then when that special day came around and you actually got the present, you were filled with excitement. Remember unwrapping the gift and lifting it up as if it were a treasure? Remember the crisp, new color? Remember playing with it? Remember the sound? Remember showing it to your friends?

This is exactly how you want to see your new life—just like a precious present selected just for you to bring you all the uninhibited childlike joy and wonder of a new bike, jacket or toy. When you see your future this way, it will happen. In contrast, if you see fear, apprehension, rejection and devastation in your future, that will happen, too.

You are at a place where you can begin to write your own story. This tale will take you to places you have never seen and give you experiences you have never felt. You are the author. Take yourself where you want to go. And know that you should be there, because you deserve it.

Recently I attended an awards ceremony for a professional who was retiring and had achieved immeasurable success in his career. He was

surely one of the most respected people in his profession whose advice
was sought nationwide. During his speech he thanked his wife, best friend
and partners as well as his colleagues and clients. Then he made what I
thought was his most profound remark: "I never applied for a job that I
was qualified for."

When he said those words, they immediately struck me. I felt exactly
the same way about my own career.

This person that we had all considered the expert of all experts actually moved along in his career not by knowing everything up front, but by
simply believing that he could *learn* quickly whatever he didn't already
know how to do. He stretched out of his comfort zone knowing that while
he might not have had all the skills, he had the confidence to take on a
new challenge and develop the skills to achieve. He felt that he could
apply the attributes that he did possess, attributes that I would describe as
character, strategic thinking skills and dedication. In my experience, these
qualities are intrinsic and not taught. We all have them. They may lay
dormant at times or have been stifled for a while. But they are there. Who
you are as a person cannot be learned in college or by reading a self-help
book. The qualities that make the greatest difference are at the very fiber
of your being. Value your qualities of kindness, patience, charitableness
and compassion. Bring those qualities to whatever you do. Show yourself
and others how your strengths lend a fresh perspective to the task at hand.
Do not dwell on what you don't know. There is a lot more that you DO
know. You already know the things that cannot be taught.

Rule Break: You need not know everything about a topic before you
can work in it. Take on a challenge for which on the surface you may not
be qualified. EXPECT that you will triumph. There are no rules that say
you will not. List what attributes you bring to the challenge that nobody
else can. If you believe that you can do it, you will find a way. What you
desire will not come to you unless you expect that it will. Be creative while
knowing that creativity is not enough. Creativity is imagining something
new. Innovation is getting it done. Be innovative.

The List of Important Things I Already Know:
1. Write, "I have organized..." and list examples of things you have
    planned over the past several years. These could include the home
    finances, a project at work, a schedule for the children's sports or

other practices, a church sale, a professional association committee, a fundraiser for a school, a family reunion.

2. Write, "I feel..." and list all the feelings you felt when you watched the movie *Bambi*, read *The Diary of Anne Frank* or dealt with something else emotional.
3. Write, "Before I die I want to..." and list ten things.
4. Write, "If my house was burning down and I could only take three things, I would take..." and list your responses. Then list "Why."
5. Write, "Nobody can take these things away from me..." and list your most valued qualities. These are things that you cannot see—sense of humor, character, creativity...
6. Write, "The last time I let somebody really help me was..." Complete this statement and then add. "It felt......"
7. Write, "The last time I really helped somebody was..." Complete this statement and then add "It felt......"

Notice that none of these has anything to do with looking back at a negative past.

Maryann's Story

Maryann Karinch knew it was not a good sign when she found out her boss from Apple Computers was coming from out of town to meet with her. Sure enough, at the age of forty, Maryann was asked to turn in her badge and leave her public relations post in Reston, Virginia, to join the ranks of the unemployed.

Many employees were being laid off as part of the company's cutbacks, but Maryann identified a luxury in her despair. As a manager she had earned five months of severance pay and eighteen months of health insurance coverage. This gave her breathing room to explore new opportunities. In her role at Apple, Maryann had promoted the company within the federal government, working mostly with Walter Reed Army Medical Center's telemedicine team. Telemedicine generally refers to the use of communications and information technologies for the delivery of clinical care. It allows patients' records and videos of procedures to be transmitted live for immediate diagnosis and follow-up treatment.

During her "meanwhile" time, Maryann had some planning to do and decided to channel her time in attending motivational seminars and listening to motivational tapes. She realized that as much as she enjoyed her work in public relations, she really wanted to be an author.

"I realized all I needed to do was to make up my mind what I really wanted, create a plan and follow through with it," said Maryann. She never expected anything but good things to happen. However, she knew to ensure that outcome, she'd need a plan. Since she had the short-term comfort of income from her severance package as well as health insurance, she decided to take the risk of pursuing her dream. She sent a query letter for a book about telemedicine to a literary agency who, in fact, asked to see the full proposal.

"I said to myself, 'I don't know how to do that,'" said Maryann, who went on to research how to write a book proposal, finished it and sent the proposal off to the agent. Within a few months she had a contract on her first book *Telemedicine: What the Future Holds When You're Ill,* which was published several months later.

"When you want something so much you will find a way," she said.

Through her journey of self-discovery Maryann was learning a lot about herself, which brought with it new changes, plans and risks. She suffered the pains of a divorce and the fears of relocating to California where, at forty-one, she took up adventure racing. She continued to write more books. Her goal was to have fifteen in print at all times. She supplemented her income with consulting in the public relations field. Maryann remarried a motivational speaker who, ironically, advises clients on how to take risks, and the two moved to Colorado.

"Our first date was a skydive," laughs Maryann, who says that challenges are very much like jumping out of an airplane. "You could die. But you prepare yourself to just have fun by the level of preparation you put in before the dive. Don't just take risks. Take intelligent risks."

The two moved to California. Today, Maryann is the author of twelve books and founder of The Rudy Agency—a literary agency she runs from her home office in Estes Park, Colorado.

"I didn't always know what I was doing but I realized that I had to plan and prepare myself as much as I possibly could," she said. "I always knew I could figure things out. You just have to do it."

Remember: List specific things you are doing to draw positive energy to your life. Envision yourself happy with a good life balance.

Exercise #19
From Rule No. 19: Expect Everything—Nothing is Gravy

The Success Quiz

	True	False
1. You are bound to fail along your journey to success.		
2. If you are having a difficult time getting started at something important, it will help if you schedule specific time to work on it when you are most alert, rested and energized.		
3. Sitting quietly for ten minutes and doing absolutely nothing but staring straight ahead or keeping your eyes closed will block your creativity.		
4. Surrounding yourself with unsuccessful people will elevate your morale and inspire success.		
5. You are on a desert island without any responsibilities such as being a parent, spouse, professional, etc. Rate yourself on a scale of one to ten with ten being the highest. People who rate themselves a ten in this exercise are more likely to succeed.		
6. The only limitations you have are those others impose on you.		
7. When charting your day, do the easiest task first.		
8. You are the reflection of the five people you associate with most and your income is the average of those five people.		
9. Things are the way you think they are, because they truly are that way. Your perception has nothing to do with your experience.		
10. Having potential simply means that you possess talents and abilities you aren't applying.		
11. Successful people expect success and they expect it now—not later. They shift and adjust their plans fifty times faster than most individuals. In some circles, they are called "movers and shakers" for good reason.		
12. Successful people always reach their goals.		
13. Successful people have a "do-it-now" philosophy.		

	True	**False**
14. The ability to "sell", whether it is yourself, a product or a service, is a key to success.		
15. The ability to bounce back from adversity is not an element of success.		
16. Most of the nervous symptoms you experience before a presentation or interview are exactly the same as those you feel when excited. To the body, adrenaline is energy whether it has been experienced in a negative or positive situation. Don't label that emotion as nervousness. Calling it excitement in your "self talk" will channel that energy to communicate joy and confidence.		
17. The enthusiasm you give to your colleagues, audiences and prospects will not be mirrored back to you.		
18. Successful people are fiscally responsible.		
19. Successful people do most of the talking in a conversation.		
20. To demonstrate a sincere interest in another person's point of view and to help understand a point and remember it better, successful people restate back what they heard a person say. "So what I hear you saying is that..."		

Answer Key:
1. True, 2. True, 3. False, 4. False, 5. True, 6. False, 7. False, 8. True, 9. False, 10. True, 11. True, 12. False, 13. True, 14. True, 15. False, 16. True, 17. False, 18. True, 19. False, 20. True.

Chapter Twenty

Rule No. 20

Make Your Mark Within Ninety Days

Okay, so by now you have allowed the world to get to know you as a problem solver who is not afraid to take on a tough challenge. They can see that you are a go-to person who is professional and results-oriented. You are intelligent, personable and have achieved a lot. The question is how soon will you be effective for your new company or client? They will not be settled until they feel they have made the right choice. You have ninety days in a new position to assure them that they have.

Many companies even have policies that allow them to fire you within ninety days without them having to implement extensive rehabilitation plans, because within this amount of time you have either been labeled a good hire or a bad hire. Most managers will tell you that they know within the first month whether or not they made the right choice. But to truly make your mark you have ninety days, so you better have a plan of action.

Also, on an interview for a management position you may be asked what your plan would be for your first ninety days so be sure to know how to answer this question.

Think about your first ninety days in your new job as you would if you were trying to build a new home in a community and needed zoning variances from the township to acquire a building permit. Would you go to community functions and introduce yourself to your new neighbors? Would you read materials to learn the history of the community? Would you introduce yourself to key public officials? Would you try to meet people of influence in the community who could help you get the needed variances? Would you enlist the support of the right professionals to design and manage the project once it was approved?

Taking a new position calls for many of the same measures.

Your First Ninety Days Plan for Leaders:

1. **Learn.** Learn as much as you can about the key service or marketing lines of an organization and the people who lead them. This learning process starts weeks before you walk into your new office. Read the annual report. Study the Web site. Ask for any materials you can review ahead of time. If you are in a leadership position, there are important things to consider as you educate yourself on the details of the organization. Meet with key people within the organization as well as your staff. Ask them all the same questions and just LISTEN:
   a.   What are the biggest challenges of the organization?
   b.   What are the most promising opportunities for the organization?
   c.   What resources are necessary to develop these opportunities?
   d.   If you were me, what would you do?

2. **Build Alliances.** You will need advisors and coalitions both inside and outside of the organization to succeed. Your sphere of influence is critical to your success. The advice you receive can save you count-less wasted hours or bad decisions. Your judgment skills will come into play here. Judge wisely. Identify key players. Those who have a strong following of effective leaders are generally strong decision makers themselves.

   Host focus groups with key leaders to get opinions on what is necessary. Ask lots of questions. Ask, "What would the ideal situation look like?" Let them do most of the talking. Write down what they say and organize the concepts into categories. Then, later ask key individ-uals if they will be an advisor or leader of a certain area.

   Ask colleagues about the organizational culture. Study what strate-gies effective leaders use to be effective in this culture.

3. **Build a Strong Relationship with Your New Boss**. Be very specific about what is expected of you so there are no surprises—how often you should meet, what he wants you to report on at those meetings, what are her goals, what you can do to help him. Allow her to know in no uncertain terms that you support 100 percent and are her go-to person

for whatever she needs. You convince him of this by delivering 110 percent on whatever he asks. And 120 percent on what she does not ask.

4. **Analyze Your Processes and Your Competitors.** Research what your competition is doing. Your goal is not to compete with them, but to develop your own niche and strategy by understanding their mission and vision and how your philosophy differs. Then further refine what problem your organization solves in your industry and the uniqueness of that process. Are there affiliated organizations from which you can learn by studying them as well? If your business sells cars, is there something that can be learned from the electronics industry? Both industries distribute nationwide, have plants that build in the United States and provide ongoing service.

5. **Build Your Internal Team.** It is important to decide early on who will fill the gaps of your internal team. If you are a manager, structure the design of your department and the qualifications that will be needed by each team member for the task at hand. Surround yourself with go-to people who positively respond to you as you respond to your boss.

6. **Engage All Stakeholders in the Difference This New Movement Will Make By Allowing Them to Own the Team's Success.** People want to be a part of a successful team. No one will help a sinking ship. They may help the passengers and crew get off the ship, but if a ship is going down, no one is interested in the ship—just helping to save the people. Define and demonstrate the vision of where you are going and the difference it will make in the lives of people, whether it is those you serve or sell to, shareholders, employees, board members or vendors in the community. Understanding people and what drives their dedication is key.

7. **Promote Early Wins.** Building some early coalitions or achieving a new feat for the company will build your momentum. Early wins help to instill credibility and faith that you will deliver what the company needs. The company does not want to worry that you won't. Be sure to communicate your wins.

Within my first ninety days in any position, I am acutely focused on how to make a difference that assures anyone associated with having hired me that he or she made the right choice. I do this by exceeding the person's expectations. This is much easier than you think if you follow the steps listed previously.

When I was the public relations director of Avonworth School District, I made sure the district had a feature in the newspaper within the first two weeks and had television coverage within the first month—two things that were non-existent until then. How did I do this? By learning everything I could about the district. By identifying the print and television media that covered school features and by regularly submitting quality items of interest to them. I met with the superintendent of schools who gave me the authority to pitch what I thought would be appropriate to the media. I read and studied everything that was being printed and aired on school districts so that I could understand what media traditionally covered. I decided that I would pitch positive feature stories about unique programs and individuals as our niche. School board meetings generated enough news already. So I enlisted the teachers to help define unique feature ideas. The stories had to be positive and unique. I made sure that I circulated a list of what had been publicized to all school board members monthly, so that our collective work was recognized. The administration and the board was supportive.

When I was the executive director of Three Rivers Advertising Spec-ialty Association, which is a trade association for the advertising specialty industry, my main goal was to grant the wishes of the board: to grow the mission of the organization by increasing business for all members. Clearly I needed to increase supplier and distributor attendance at the annual trade show. The economic denominator was supplier participation, because suppliers paid a hefty price for their booth spaces. I knew that increased supplier participation would increase income. This would also grow the association's ability to provide strong educational programs with well known speakers.

First, I engaged the support of dedicated supplier members to help me define suppliers that exhibit at other shows who were not at ours. Then, I created a package whereby suppliers could exhibit at a show in a nearby town and piggyback in doing our show two days later. Many of the suppliers had not heard of our show before then, but since it was close to where they were already exhibiting and the price was right, they did ours as well. Knowing that we had a dramatic increase in supplier participation, we launched a full marketing plan to distributors with continual mass e-mails and faxes, underscoring the increasing list of suppliers.

The results were that distributor attendance increased 150 percent, membership increased 30 percent and income increased 60 percent. The Association won the industry's national "Association of the Year Award" that year. Additionally, my compensation increased dramatically, because there was now income to warrant the increase. Additionally, we had a lot of fun doing it. The experience built relationships that last to this day. Build experience and you build relationships.

Remember: Make sure to follow the First Ninety Day Plan in order to secure a strong first impression with your new employer.

Exercise #20
From Rule No. 20: Make Your Mark Within Ninety Days

Steps for Your First Ninety Days

Whether your have begun a new job or are starting a new frontier in your existing job, answer these questions to make sure you are making executive management nod their heads. If you answer "No" to any of these questions, know that your plan to make some changes begins today, not next week.

My First Ninety Days...	Yes	No
1. Did you mark a giant X on your office calendar on the 90th day after you started?		
2. Do you show up early and stay late?		
3. Do you accept every invitation you get for meetings, coffee, lunch or dinner as people extend themselves to you?		
4. Do you focus on building relationships? Call people for opinions and lunch?		
5. Do you get to know the culture by asking people what they think the company strengths and weaknesses are?		
6. Did you ask lots of thoughtful questions at meetings and off-line?		
7. Do you ask for feedback? (Without defensiveness. Just listen and nod.)		
8. Do you make no rash decisions?		
9. Do you refrain from gossip about anyone?		
10. Do you greet everyone you pass with "Hello!" or "Good morning?"		
11. Fifteen minutes before you leave work, do you plan what your next day will look like?		
12. Are you known for you honesty and integrity?		
13. Do you talk 20 percent of the time and listen 80 percent of the time?		
14. Without exception, do you show respect for your boss?		
15. When you are complimented, do you share the credit with the team?		
16. Do you keep your personal life out of the office?		
17. Do you ask you boss periodically if there is something on which he/she thinks you should be working or refocusing?		
18. Do you compliment your co-workers?		
19. Have you read the company's annual report?		
20. Have you read your competitors' annual reports?		
21. Have you found a mentor within the organization?		
22. Have you made constructive and well thought-out suggestions on how to solve a problem to those above you?		
23. Are you conscious of your health? Exercise regularly? Eat well? Limit junk food?		

Chapter Twenty-One

Rule No. 21

Start Every Day As if It Were the Last Day Before Vacation

Think about the last time you packed up the car and headed for your favorite travel destination. The day before you left you had to organize your clothes and possibly those of others to fit neatly in a cramped suitcase. You had to make a list and stock up on food and items you'd need while away. You had to pay your bills and take care of things that would happen in your absence, such as postponing the mail or newspaper delivery. Think of what you'd accomplish if you experienced every day with the same strategy, vigor and follow-through as the day before you left for vacation.

You are on a new quest. You are pursuing something in your life that you haven't done before. This is a special opportunity for you to accomplish something new and big. Nobody can do this well without being organized.

If you are starting this quest from home, prepare a special place in your home with the tools you will need to succeed in this new quest and where you will find it a pleasure to work. If you are starting this journey while employed, you still may want to organize a home office for better life balance.

Locate a permanent place within your home for your office. A separate room is ideal. Try to keep this space out of your bedroom. You need a relaxing night's sleep away from any stressors in your life. Put a photo of the most important people in your life within sight of your work area to remind you of the support you have.

If your office is at home and you do not have a separate room for it, you can use a screen or a curtain to set off a corner of a room and create an office space. Find a hidden-away nook that will be free from interruptions. Use a roll-down window blind to enclose the office when not in use. Mount shelves above the desk for extra space and use a foldaway table for extra workspace when needed.

Phone access is important. If you will be using your cell phone and wireless Internet, you need not worry about a phone jack. However, if you are using a landline, make sure a jack is close by or call your phone company to have one installed.

Whether in a home office or an office outside of the home, select some furniture that is within your budget. If you are purchasing something new, an L-shaped arrangement is preferred as it will allow you space to organize papers while you are working. Used office furniture will work as well. It need not be perfect or new; just apart from distractions and specifically dedicated to your adventure.

You will need a computer and printer. Position your monitor sixteen to thirty inches away from your eyes, depending on what's comfortable. Ideally, the monitor should be four to eight inches lower than eye level, so you're looking slightly down towards it and tilted slightly up, as if it were a book. A laptop computer accomplishes this most easily. If you're shopping for a monitor, look for one with a high pixel count and a high refresh rate. Pixels are the colored dots that make up an image; a higher refresh rate means fewer flickers on your screen.

A home office is now considered a principal place of business if it is used for substantial managerial or administrative tasks such as scheduling appointments, keeping business books and records and ordering or storing supplies. Check with your tax consultant or research to see if deducting your home office is appropriate for you.

The desk items you use most often, such as a phone, a book or business card holder should be placed within easy view or access. You do not want to have to excessively twist or bend your body while using these items. Excessive reaching takes time and doing so in the sitting position can strain your body.

A light source should be placed perpendicular to your computer, so it will not shine in your eyes or reflect on your screen. If you're typing from documents, keep them as close to your monitor as possible so you don't have to swivel to gaze back and forth.

When typing, it is best to keep your wrists in a neutral position. Abnormal positions can place undue strain on the forearm muscles and upper arms and shoulders, which anchor to the upper body and neck, which can make them sore.

An organized office does not make an organized worker. In order to create new outcomes for yourself, you need to create new habits. Have your old habits served you well? Consider a different way of structuring your day.

In 1906 Vilfredo Pareto, an Italian economist, discovered that 80 percent of the land in Italy (and every country he studied) was owned by 20 percent of the population. Pareto's theory of predictable imbalance has since been applied to almost every aspect of modern life. Simply put, the 80/20 rule states that the relationship between input and output is rarely, if ever, balanced. 80 percent of the wealth was held by 20 percent of the people. Essentially this means: 20 percent of a sales force produces 80 percent of a company's revenues; 80 percent of delays in schedule arise from 20 percent of the possible causes of the delays; 80 percent of customer complaints arise from 20 percent of products or services.

When you have your office set up the way you want it, you will want to manage your time to be most efficient, so that nearly 100 percent of the time you are working on things that bring about the greatest return. You do not want to spend your day answering e-mails and talking on the phone, which does not get you a new job or improved profits. You want to spend time networking via phone from your office, gaining the mentors that will help you get closer to your dreams.

As I've told you when I launched my career change, my four children were under seven years old, one of whom was an infant. I have found that being able to apply the 80/20 rule to my work is a secret to my achievements even today. I started my day taking Maria and Brianna to elementary school and Andrea to preschool. Then Max and I came home and enjoyed some playtime until he took a morning nap. As he napped, I worked on a marathon of projects until he awoke: I'd interview someone over the phone for a newspaper story, contact a television station to pitch a story for my public school district client, open the mail and log eight more booths into the database of trade show participants for my association client. I picked up Andrea from preschool midday and repeated the marathon work process during Max and Andrea's afternoon nap.

I had to be organized, because my time was limited. If I had a business meeting scheduled often Max came with me. My boss and colleagues in the advertising specialty industry always welcomed Max in the office. You know and appreciate the angels in your life. In the summers, I took the children to the pool during the day and worked at night. Some say I had a hectic life. I appreciated the freedom of being able to be home with my children when they were young; I was grateful.

If traditionally 20 percent of your efforts produce 80 percent of the results, learn to recognize and then focus more than 20 percent of your work on what will bring you closest to your goals and do those things *first*. Make sure you are working on the things that bring about the greatest return.

Let me give you an example as it relates to fundraising. Many fundraising organizations spend a lot of time focusing on annual direct mail appeals and special events. These are key elements in a fundraising plan, because these programs are where organizations acquire new donors and promote their missions. Depending on the organization, many of these new donors will not renew their donations or event participation the following year. This means that organizations must continue to repeatedly throw out the net in creative and innovative ways to capture new donors. The goal is to develop relationships with these new donors over time so that they increase their giving and become major gift donors.

Direct mail and special events are costly to operate. They require an inordinate number of skilled people working long hours to manage components such as data, mailing audiences, return mail coding, print material design and reservations among other tasks. They require a large budget to pay for postage, printing, mail sorting, decorations, staging, etc. The return on investment is low as compared to major gift solicitation work.

So why do non-profits focus mostly on these methods? It's because it is easier to find people to do this work than it is to find people to comb through the annual fund donor list and systematically sit down with individual donors over time and engage them in a face-to-face discussion on making a major gift. It is easier to manage the finite data of mailing lists and event participants than it is to methodically build a major gifts program that takes prospect research, development of staff, accountability of that staff and the higher likelihood of their collective burnout.

Truth be told, most non-profit organizations have a host of major gift prospects within their own donor database but have not been able to define or develop them because they are too busy with more predictable but less productive programs. It is human nature to gravitate toward what is familiar.

Put the 80/20 rule to work for you. Are you using 80 percent of your time on what will bring you or your company the greatest return? If not, what change do you need to make to upset that ratio? If you don't, you will not be noticed.

Rule Break: Don't start your day with a "to do" list. Start every day as if it were the day before you go on vacation. Make sure things will be working for you in your absence by creating a checklist. Decide what things need to be put in place now so that they will pay off in the near future. Figure out what you want to return to if you are gone for two weeks.

You need not have fancy office furniture with color coordinated desk accessories to move your life forward. You do need a dedicated space and an organizational prioritization system to do so.

How to Organize and Prioritize:

1. *Keep a calendar.* Either get a hard copy weekly or monthly calendar that can be purchased at any discount or office supply store or use a software program that keeps your calendar on your computer and/or links it to your phone. Run off hard copies and scan your week and your month for better planning.

2. *Create a "Valued Friends" list of the names of people with whom you have met at networking and other social events that you learned about in chapter 9.* Keep a record of the date of the meeting, what was discussed and the "next action" you will take to build the relationship. Many people keep this information in a spreadsheet such as Excel or in a database such as Access. Either become familiar with these programs, keep a hard copy list or keep the list alphabetically in a word processing document.

3. *Be sure to mark your calendar with the "next action" from step two and a timeline.* That action should include something that will be of benefit to them.

4. *Make a list of your daily tasks and compare it to your five year goals.* Then rank everything in your task list as either a one, two or three in terms of what will get you closer to your five-year goals. Make sure that 80 percent of your day is spent doing things in the first category. That equals 6.4 hours of an eight-hour day. The rest is secondary.

5. *Answer phone messages and e-mails at the end of the day after you have done the work that is going to bring you closest to your goals.*

Remember: Stay ahead of your work schedule to ensure success.

Exercise #21
From Rule No. 21: Start Every Day As If It Were the Last Day Before Vacation

The 80/20 Rule Checklist

80 percent of the results come from 20 percent of the work. Answer these questions "Yes" and you know you are working smart. If your answer is "No", then what is your plan to switch this around?

	Yes/No
Are you working on tasks that solve big problems?	
Are you working on tasks that are urgent for your area's results and not what is urgent for someone else's results?	
Are you advancing activities that are getting you closer to your five-year goals?	
Are you feeling positive as opposed to overwhelmed and complaining?	
Is your work challenging you and stretching your talent as opposed to being work you are very comfortable with?	
Are you doing things you always wanted to do?	
Are you working on tasks you don't like but know they relate to the big picture?	
Are you surrounding yourself with people whose strengths are your weaknesses?	

The 80/20 Work List

It is probable that we waste lots of time on trivial, repetitive tasks that keep us busy but are not productive. Equipment is running whether needed or not, sales are made whether they are profitable or not, files are being moved from one station to another whether or not all stations are necessary. Which tasks can be eliminated, delegated or streamlined so that you may get on to the work that produces the greatest results?

Daily Work Task	Percentage of my time?	80 percent activity?	Eliminate or delegate?
1. Daily Work Task:			
2. Daily Work Task:			
3. Daily Work Task:			
4. Daily Work Task:			
5. Daily Work Task:			
6. Problem Solving:		Yes	
7. Process Redesign: (which ones?)		Yes	
8. Complimenting Others:		Yes	
9. Reviewing Our Results/Journals/Competition's Reports:		Yes	
10. Strategic Planning:		Yes	

Chapter Twenty-Two

Rule No. 22

Know Which Glass is Yours and Take a New Friend to Lunch

Offer to take your mentor to lunch as you build your relationship. You may be invited to lunch with some new friends. You may be attending a Chamber of Commerce, Rotary or other business networking event that includes lunch. Make sure whatever the event, you project the professional person you are. Bad table manners are inexcusable in business. They project a person that has not reached a sophisticated level of accomplishment. A person who is accomplished would know which glass is his or hers. So be sure to brush up on table etiquette during your "meanwhile" time.

Employers may want to see you in a more social situation to see how you conduct yourself, particularly if the job for which you are interviewing requires a certain standard of conduct with clients and superiors. A lunch or dinner is a time to visit and interact, and this is always more important than the function of eating. Understand that your prospective employer will be observing your social grace, your manners and your ease in this situation.

There are a variety of rules on dining etiquette in both the American and European styles, which can be learned from books you will find at the library or bookstore. For practical purposes I will stick to the basics here.

When you sit down at a table that is set to serve many guests, often it is difficult to remember which butter plate and which glass of water is yours. There are two very easy principals to remember here. Liquids are on the right, solids are on the left. All glasses and coffee cups on the right will be yours. That means that all solids—the butter and salad plate as well as the napkin on the left—are yours. Hot beverages are stirred with a spoon that is also on the right. Your salad plate is on the left as is the salad fork.

Proper posture at the table is very important. Sit up straight, with your arms held near your body. You should neither lean on the back of the chair nor bend forward to place your elbows on the table. When eating, you should be two hand widths away from the table. Elbows never go on the table. Wrists can rest on the side of the table or in your lap. No matter what the situation, you never complain about the food.

Typically, you want to unfold your napkin and put it on your lap soon after sitting down at the table. However, if you are a guest, follow your host's lead. When the host unfolds his or her napkin, this is your signal to do the same. The napkin remains on your lap throughout the entire meal. Gently blot your mouth when needed. If you need to leave the table during the meal, excuse yourself and place your napkin on your chair as a signal to your server that you will be returning. Place the handles of your silverware at 3:00 with the other ends pointing to the center to indicate that you are not finished. Men should rise when a woman leaves the table. It is not necessary to rise all the way; partway is sufficient.

Sometimes if he or she does not verbally indicate it, the host will signal that the meal has ended by placing his or her napkin on the table. Once the meal is over, you too should place your napkin neatly on the table to the right of your dinner plate. Your silverware should be placed at 4:00 pointing to 10:00 always with the blade pointed toward you.

If you are at a restaurant, do not order one of the most expensive items on the menu or more than two courses unless your host indicates that it is acceptable. If the host says, "I'm going to order the dark chocolate cake; please feel free to order dessert," or "The Virginia Spots is the house special; I think you'd enjoy it," then it is all right to order that item if you would like. Do not order an alcoholic drink during a workday event and do not ever smoke at the table.

Order simple foods that are easily eaten with a fork and knife (meats, simple salads and soups). Avoid pasta or other things with red sauce, sandwiches that can fall apart or get on your clothes when you eat them and greasy handheld items like pizza. Follow your host's lead.

The simple rule for silverware is to work from the outside in. The fork on the outside is your salad fork. Your dessert spoon and fork are above your plate or brought out with dessert. Glasses are on the right and follow the same rule of progression. The wine glass will be on the outside. Red wine glasses will have a larger bowl then white wine glasses. White wine glasses should be held from the stem so as not to warm the chilled wine. Red wine is served at room temperature and the glass may be held by the bowl since the heat from your hand will not affect the taste. The water glass will be farthest to the left. Do not crush ice with your teeth.

The soup spoon will be on your far right and should enter the bowl and be scooped away from you. Hold the spoon with your thumb on the top of the handle. Sip silently from the side of the spoon and do not put the entire spoon in your mouth. If your soup came on a service plate, leave the spoon on the plate when you take a break from eating or when you are finished. If your soup came in a bowl without a service plate, leave the spoon in the bowl when taking a break and when finished.

If you are served crackers, do not break crackers into your soup. Put the spoon down, break off a piece if it is a large cracker and eat it. Do the same with bread. Break off a piece of bread, butter it and, if you wish, put the remaining piece down before you eat the buttered piece. Do not bite into bread or a roll. If there is not a butter knife on your butter plate, you may use the dinner knife but place it on your butter plate until your meal is served—then move it over. Do not mop your plate with a piece of bread. The sharp part of knives should always face you when resting on the plate.

Be sure to cut your food with the fork in your left hand facing down on your plate and the handle tucked under the palm of your hand. Use your pointer finger to control it. The knife will cut from side to side just behind the fork, again with the handle tucked into the palm of your right hand and the knife controlled by your pointer finger. Keep those handles under your palms! Place the knife down at the top of the plate with the sharp edge facing you before you take a bite. As you take a bite, transition the handle of the fork to between your pointer finger and your thumb.

There are more dining etiquette rules to remember. Generally, if you remember left-to-right you will be fine. You will be served from the left and plates will be removed from the right. When you sit down, take your chair from the left and excuse yourself from the right. Pass things to your right. If you are asked to pass the salt, be sure to pass both the salt and pepper together. No purses or other items should be placed on the table. The general rule for removing unwanted food, such as gristle, from your mouth is that it should go out the same way it went in—on a fork or spoon.

Place the piece of food on the edge of your plate. If you used your fingers to put an olive into your mouth that was part of an hors d'oeuvre tray, then you may remove it with your fingers. Any utensil that has been used should not touch the table again; it should remain on the plate.

When you are finished eating, place your fork tines down in front of the knife, blade toward you, at the 10:00 and 4:00 positions. This will indicate to the staff that you have finished eating and they can remove your plate.

In conclusion, remember to work from the outside in regarding silverware. Liquids on your right, solids on your left and everything passes from left to right.

Rule Break: There are foods that may be carefully eaten with your fingers. These include: artichokes, bacon, bread, hors d'oeuvres, sandwiches, cookies, small fruits or berries with stems, french fries and potato chips, hamburgers and hot dogs, corn on the cob and pickles.

Nine Rules of Dining Etiquette:

1. **Your Host:** Take your lead from the host. When he sits down to eat you sit down. When she puts her napkin on her lap, you do the same. If he orders dessert, you may as well, etc.
2. **Napkin:** In general, your napkin goes on your lap when you sit down, on your chair when you excuse yourself from the table and on the table to the right of the plate when you are finished.
3. **Liquids:** Liquids (glasses and coffee cup) are placed on the right.
4. **Solids:** Solids (bread and butter plate, salad plate and napkin) are placed on the left.
5. **Vices:** Do not order an alcoholic beverage or smoke at a business lunch.
6. **Utensils:** Work from the outside in with utensils. The salad fork is on the outside to the left as the salad is served first. The soup spoon is on the outside to the right or may be brought with the soup.
7. **Bread:** Break and butter only the piece of bread you will put in your mouth. Do not put the entire roll in your mouth and take a bite.
8. **Cutting:** Cut your food with the fork in your left hand and the knife in your right, both with the handles under your palms and directing the utensils with your pointer fingers. The knife cuts behind the fork.

Put down the knife at the top of the plate, blade toward you, when you take a bite. Position the fork tines up when you eat.

9. **Finished:** When you are finished eating, put the knife, blade toward you, to the right of the fork with its tines down diagonally lying from the 10:00 to the 4:00 positions on the plate.

Three Simple Rules to Put Good Manners to Use with Your Mentor:
1. Take your mentor or a new friend to lunch once a month.
2. Always pay.
3. Send that friend a follow-up note on how much you enjoyed the lunch and appreciate his or her guidance. Include a tip or information that can help the person in an area of interest to him or her.

Remember: Having proper table manners is essential when dining with business partners and associates.

Exercise #22
From Rule No. 22: Know Which Glass is Yours
and Take a New Friend to Lunch

Dining Etiquette Quiz

If you follow the "Nine Rules of Dining Etiquette" and pass this quiz, you are ready for a five-star restaurant or a simple lunch with your mentor.

1. I have asked my mentor to lunch and she has agreed. She has an executive level position. When the check comes she offers to pay. What do I do?

2. You were invited to an interview over lunch. The food was not hot and the fish was barely cooked. Your host asks how your meal was. You respond:

3. Onions are served with a salad and you don't want to eat them. What do you do?

4. You find that you have a bone or something unpalatable in your mouth. Do you take it out with your fingers and put it on the tablecloth?

5. You have dropped your fork on the floor. Do you pick it up?

6. Where do you place the knife when you are eating?

7. Is it ever okay to remove your suit jacket for heat or other reasons? Does this differ for males and females?

8. If a lady were to get up during the meal, should all men get up too?

9. Is it rude to season your food before you taste it?

10. Should the host of a business meal take the best seat?

ANSWERS:
1. In business if you invite someone to lunch, you pay. Period.
2. "It was fine, thank you!" Never complain about anything. If the food is inedible, graciously summon the server and explain.
3. You eat around them. You do not remove them from the plate.
4. No. Take it out with the utensil that fed it to your mouth and put it on the side of your plate.
5. No. You leave it and ask the server for another. The same goes for food dropped on the floor.
6. Put the knife across the top of your plate when you are eating, blade facing toward you.
7. Keep in mind that some restaurants/clubs require customers to keep their jackets on during meals. As a general rule, follow the lead of the host before removing your jacket. If the host keeps on his or her jacket, keep yours on. It is appropriate to ask the host or hostess permission if the room is very hot. This applies to both men and women.
8. Yes. Men should rise when a lady leaves the table. It is not necessary to completely stand for a temporary departure. Simply rise off the seat to acknowledge her leaving.
9. Yes. It is an insult to the chef to season food before you try a bite.
10. No. The host should always take the worst seat. The guest of honor should always take the best seat. The best seat generally allows the best view of the room and other diners.

Chapter Twenty-Three

Rule No. 23

Dedication Trumps Motivation

How many mornings have you awakened and said to yourself, "I just am not motivated to do anything today"? Probably many. How many mornings have you awakened and said to yourself, "I am just not dedicated to anything today"? Probably none.

How many times have you read a book or gone to a lecture and left feeling invigorated, only to discover that a few days later you were back to feeling the same way as before—not motivated to make change or do anything differently? Or how many times have you attended a great lecture or seminar only to return to your office, start opening e-mails and never actually executed the principals you've learned? Probably plenty. You were probably waiting for the invigorated feeling that was present at the conference to stay with you and it did not. Motivation always needs to be reignited.

There are things to which you are dedicated that are unwavering. If a child offended your daughter, you would probably be motivated to help your child understand that no matter what anyone says, you love her and nobody can change that. If it was a serious problem you might talk to the parents. You'd help your child focus on the good friends that she has. On the other hand, if an adult physically assaulted your child, you would probably report it to the police and/or school. Would you sit around saying to yourself, "I'm just not motivated to do that today?" I think not.

It is the same with your career. You may not know exactly what career will be calling you but you will go further in your career knowing that whatever you do, you will do whatever it takes to accomplish what you want, no matter what. If you are not sure what you want to pursue as a career, spend your "meanwhile" time reading everything you can about identifying your strengths and thinking about what you love to do.

Eliminate "can't" from your vocabulary. It means "won't." You have big dreams of what you'd like to do and where you'd like to be. However, there is some reason you "can't" get there. You don't have enough education or enough money. You don't know how or don't have time with all the needs of your children. As long as you validate "can't" in your vocabulary, the reasons why you "can't" will continue to run over and over in your mind like a broken record. Tell yourself that you "can." The reasons why you "can" will start running over and over in your mind and then you will find that you "will." Trust me on this one.

Also in your dedication, be able to identify when it is time to move on to greater challenges. If you do not, you may become stagnant, which will not help to further propel you up the ladder to your goals. In your current position, if you find you are simply repeating the same work you did the year before with no greater challenge, it is time to move on. How else will you acquire more skills to improve your problem solving abilities?

When I left my first position as the executive director of a hospital foundation to go to a larger foundation, it was not because I was unhappy in my first position. I loved my job, the people I worked with and my boss - still a good friend today—but I realized that I was not able to take on greater challenges there because of the size and breadth of the institution. So, I took on a position with larger responsibility.

Dedication is part of who you are and does not need to be reignited like motivation does.

We've discussed the period when my children were very young and I was able to be a stay-at-home mother dedicated to their health and well-being. During this time I discovered that our family was paying a very high insurance premium, as my husband was self-employed and not part of larger group coverage. We also paid an unbelievably high co-pay every time I took the children to the doctor's office. Healthcare for my family was becoming cost prohibitive. Because of my dedication to my children's needs and my fear of how these costs were affecting other families, I wrote a letter to then-First Lady Hilary Clinton, who was championing a healthcare bill on Capital Hill just after her husband Bill was inaugurated as president. It took me an afternoon to compose the letter, and yes it was difficult to find the time with the duties for four small children. But I thought it was important for her to know that I went to fill a prescription for a sample size amount of eye ointment—a size we had given away in the ophthalmologist's office where I had worked as a certified ophthalmic technician in my twenties. The cost of this one-and-a-half-inch sample size tube was thirty-two dollars. "Where is the competition in the pharmaceutical industry?" I asked.

Two months later I got a call from the White House. "Mrs. Clinton would like to use your story on Capital Hill if that is okay with you." Okay? I was honored.

Two weeks later, I got a call that the White House was sending a photographer to my house to photograph my four children and me. I couldn't believe it.

A few weeks later, I got another call from the White House in which the caller asked permission for the Small Business Administration to analyze how much Mrs. Clinton's proposal would save my husband's business on health insurance costs. My husband agreed and they did the analysis. The plan would have saved his business thousands of dollars. After that we were invited to the White House Rose Garden for the president and Mrs. Clinton's public debut of the plan. As I met Mrs. Clinton in the Rose Garden I asked myself, "Did I ever think that my letter would gain this response?" The answer was a resounding, "No."

My dedication to a cause I felt strongly about resulted in a return way beyond what I could have imagined. I didn't ask myself, "Am I motivated to write this letter?" I just did it.

You can utilize the same approach. Just do it.

A few summers after my meeting with President and Mrs. Clinton, I took my children to Washington, D.C., to visit my brother and his family. To our surprise the brochure with our photo was mounted on the wall of the Smithsonian Institution as part of a display that was dedicated to Mrs. Clinton. I guess you could say we are in the Smithsonian. I'd prefer to say the cause I championed is in the Smithsonian.

Rule Break: Don't wait to feel motivated to get started at what you love. Define what you love, even if the definition is not as complete as you want it to be, and start doing more of it regularly. You may love to write. Keep a journal every day. You may love to help people and love children. Make a call to an agency that interests you. You may love to organize. Start with your utensils drawer in the kitchen.

Four Steps to Define What You Love to Do:
1. As a child, when you were in that very special place that you loved more than anything (the beach, your room, the attic, the park, your grandparents' house, a friend's family room, etc.), what was it that you loved to pretend?
2. When you were young, what was the one thing you liked to do more than anything else? What else did you like to do?
3. Before you go to bed at night take a pad of paper and a pen or pencil and write down, "I love to_____," or "I am happiest when _____" Do this every night until something real starts to take shape in your mind.
4. Just do it.

   Remember: Always follow through on the goals you set for yourself.

Exercise #23
From Rule No. 23: Dedication Trumps Motivation

The Dedication Quiz

1. Your alarm goes off and you hear your favorite song on the radio.
   a) You stay in bed and listen. It is only three minutes.
   b) You get up, knowing you can download the song and listen to it later. You have work to do and problems to solve.

2. You are doing consulting work for an organization and they ask you to do some work outside of your contract.
   a) You say that you are happy to do that work and will submit a proposal with detailed costs for consideration within five days.
   b) You say that although the work is outside of the scope of your agreement, because of your existing working relationship you would like to offer some preliminary background work on the issue with no fee attached so that they may make a meaningful decision on whether or not to engage in further work.

3. Your boss asks you to organize a project by Friday for which you have very little background.
   a) You state that you don't know a lot about that type of work but that you will do the best you can and have it to him by Friday.
   b) You agree and immediately contact your mentors who have experience in that area and ask them how they would proceed. Then you gather all the data that your mentors recommended, do some research of your own and organize it all into a report that shows strategies that solve problems with measurable outcomes. You hand it in on Thursday.

4. You contact the office of Nancy, a prospective client whose name you were given by a colleague. Nancy is not in.
   a) You leave a message that you have a mutual friend and hope that Nancy will call you back.
   b) You call back only to find an answering machine message. You keep calling until you finally reach her assistant. You ask her assistant's name (Kim) and tell Kim that you were given Nancy's name by a mutual friend, Dave Thomas, because you were able to help him (grow sales, reduce costs, increase productivity). "Before I take up any of Nancy's time or yours, Kim, I am just wondering if reducing costs is an issue that you are dealing with right now. Since I was able to reduce costs for Nancy's friend, Dave, he thought it might make sense for us to have a ten minute conversation on whether XYZ Company has the potential to achieve the same results."

5. A big company event is going to occur this evening. As you are setting up the event you
    realize that the printed program has key sponsors listed incorrectly. There is not time to
    reprint.
    a) You decide to make an announcement from the podium that night to give special recog-
    nition to the sponsors who were incorrectly listed.
    b) You go back to your office and print off table tents on card stock that correctly list all the
    key sponsors and place them on all of the tables. You also make an announcement from
    the podium that night to give special recognition to all the sponsors. You recognize later
    that you made an error in the program and offer a discount on the evening or on a future
    sponsorship package.

ANSWERS:
    Obviously if you have answered "b" to these questions, you understand the difference
between motivation and dedication. Dedication is a mind-set that you will do whatever it takes
to achieve the best outcome possible. You will become the "go to" person. You will be in a
position of power.

Chapter Twenty-Four

Rule No. 24

Don't Go to the Mall— Go to Computer and Other Classes

One of the most difficult challenges you experience going through a life transition is deciding where it is you should be headed. You still don't have a clear vision of what direction you want to take. You have a lot of energy and you want to get started at something new, but you don't quite know what new thing you should be doing. You have spent a lot of time being unhappy and now you are willing to do something about it, but you just don't know what.

During this "meanwhile" stage, make good use of your spare time. Once you launch on your new journey, you will be too busy to get some of the foundation tools you will need along the way. Many community college and community education programs offer scholarships on these subjects. Get some catalogs and brochures. Look for courses and lectures that will fill in gaps, then apply.

When I was in my "meanwhile" period, I decided to learn every computer software program I could and that I would need to succeed. If you are going to work in any business, being proficient in basic Microsoft Office software is essential. I taught myself how to use these programs, but there are basic courses at community colleges that will make this process easier and quicker for you.

If you want to be able to write effective letters and other documents, keep data and manipulate data for mailing purposes, mastering Microsoft Word, Excel and Access will enable you to do these things. If you go on an interview and do not have these skills, most likely you will be at a disadvantage.

If you are seeking out new learning opportunities, understand that today's requirements for learning are much different than in the past. In the elementary, high school or even college classroom decades ago, there was a lot of education that was not always applicable to day-to-day lives. You now need specific single-concept knowledge that can be applied to make better decisions that lead to interesting employment and a more fulfilling life. No fluff; just practical content in a diverse and eclectic atmosphere.

Because you've experienced a changing event, you must seek out useful and relevant knowledge. The more life changing events encountered, the more likely a person should find learning opportunities in order to better cope and move beyond despair. As you're aware, stress increases as life changing events increase, but so must one's desire to better deal with change.

I've found that many people prefer self-directed and self-designed learning projects over group learning experiences led by a teacher. More than one medium for learning is good, as well as being able to control pace and start/stop time. Seek programs designed to accept viewpoints from people in different life stages and with different value "sets." Seek learning situations where concepts are explained from more than one value set with appeal to more than one developmental life stage. Many educators recognize the different needs of the adult learner. Look for an adult classroom that will welcome and adapt to your needs.

For instance, if you want to learn how to have better sales techniques, now is the time to take a course. Once you start selling, you may be too busy to spend as much time on your craft. Be a lifelong learner. Concentrate on non-fiction.

You might say, "I am already busy." You're right. You already are. But are you using the 80/20 rule and spending your time on the things that bring about the greatest return? Most likely there is something in your life that has to be eliminated, and shopping is the easiest thing to delete. Why? Because studying a new skill will not only serve your future better, it will also save you money.

Most people enjoy shopping, because it is a very easy thing to do. You go to the mall, you walk from store to store. You admire what is there and dream of what it might be like to have it. You have a little money in your bank account or worse yet, credit available to you, so you buy stuff. Then you take what you bought home and wear it someplace where you will also probably spend more money. Or you use what you bought in some way that also may require another purchase.

Endless consumption will get you nowhere and the instant gratifica-tion will flitter out before the end of the day you use your new purchase.

Studying, reading and learning are much harder and infinitely more interesting and long lasting. Once you have studied and learned informa-tion, you have it with you to bring you gratification forever. This far outweighs buying a new shirt that will be faded or wash-worn before next season.

When you start reading and studying, you will want to keep learning more and more. You will open a door and there will be another door you want to open. So you will read and study more things as you become a life-long learner.

If you are pursuing a particular field that requires a certification, now is the time to study for that certification, because when you start your new career you may be too busy. I prepared for my certification—Certified Association Executive—during my "meanwhile." I had been managing a small association in the advertising specialty industry, which was a part-time position I did from my home office. In this position I increased trade show attendance 150 percent and broke every record the association ever had. Yet I wanted more of a challenge. Since I was self-employed, I used some of my time to prepare for the certification exam. That exam ended up being the most worthwhile thing I ever pursued. Make your "mean-while" meaningful.

Studying for this certification and attending study groups was difficult, because I was juggling writing for the newspaper, working with all my pri-vate clients and coping with the most trying part of my divorce. But it was worth it to me because the process gave me a lot more than a certificate. I was able to mentor under professionals who are masters at management and have grown to become lifelong friends with each of them.

As I prepared for the test, I was faced with an unexpected setback. Seven days before the four-hour examination I awoke with pounding chest pain, tingling in my finger and the sweats. I couldn't make it down the steps so I called for my daughter Maria, eleven years old at the time, crawled back in bed and dialed 911. I explained my symptoms to the dis-patcher and as any healthy forty-year-old would do, immediately went into denial.

"It's not that bad. I'm young. Don't you think I'll be okay?"

"We don't know that, ma'am," he said. "Have someone turn on your porch light. We'll be right there."

Just what you want to hear when you are having a tug of war with middle age: "ma'am." I wanted to tell him, "I'm not your mother," but I thought I'd better not argue.

The ambulance crew asked me if I had been under stress lately. I laughed.

Standing around my bed were my children, whose faces had dropped. I did my best to comfort and assure them, tears swelling in their eyes as the ambulance pulled away from the house.

I truly believed I would be all right and didn't get concerned until they told me at the hospital that I needed to be taken to another hospital for a heart catheterization. Then they told me I had to go by helicopter.

"Could I die?" I asked the cardiologist.

"If you weren't here it could be a possibility," he answered.

I looked at the nurse. My face must have told the story. "Please don't cry or I'm going to cry too," she said.

The sights and sounds of an emergency room during a crisis remind you of what life really amounts to. There is no sense of day or night. The words of nearby conversations pale to beeping monitors. Intravenous tubes feed what you hope is tomorrow into your veins. There are no windows through which you can breathe fresh air. And no horizon from which you can anticipate the next sunrise. There is only today. This minute. Now.

I thought about my children and how proud I am of their choices. I thought about the friends I am so blessed to have. I called my family, friends and school officials to make sure they knew to take care of the children.

Then I let God have the rest.

I knew that in spite of the difficult hand I had been dealt, I had so many things for which to give thanks. I had great care, cutting edge technology, the fastest transportation and I believed in a God who would not abandon me. Everything else was out of my hands.

As I was coming out of sedation, I watched the monitors display the movement of blood through my heart. I sighed with relief when I heard the cardiologist say with an Irish accent, "Mary, you are not having a heart attack. How do you feel?"

I answered in a very Tony the Tiger-like voice, "Grrrrrrrreeeeeeeeat!"

He smiled. "We only give the best cocktails here."

I was sure they only gave the best of everything.

After I returned home, I had a decision to make. Would I ask to be allowed to take the examination at its next sitting, which was six months later? All my friends suggested I do so. Or would I go ahead and take the exam in seven days. Knowing how much I disliked studying for tests I decided to take the examination as scheduled. That week all my friends, even my clients who I realized then were friends stopped by with books on relaxation, CDs of ocean waves pounding on the sand, tapes of rain in the forest, candles and incense. I could have opened a shop.

I truly had so much to appreciate and took that energy with me to take the exam, which I passed. With all those good feelings around me, how could I not?

Rule Break: Going back to school or college may be the route you want to take. This requires strict discipline and finances or borrowing ability to accomplish. For some professions it may be critical. I do not believe it is necessary to go back to college to start your life over without having to start at the bottom. Remember, get the basic computer skills that you need to be an asset to any business, even your own. Be able to write documents, enter data and eventually be able to analyze and manipulate data to start opening doors to be a problem solver for any business. Then become a lifelong learner. Read, then read some more.

If you are not sure what you want to study, take a course on something that you always loved as a child, just to become familiar with the classroom environment. I have taken a lot of what I call "just because" classes over the years and still do. Subjects have ranged from baking with chocolate, to French, to home repairs, to Greek cooking, to Yoga. And I have taken a lot of professional non-credit courses as well, including Pagemaker, Photoshop, Networking as well as having attended hundreds of professional conferences.

Love to learn. Learning will love you. There will be no end to what you will find out.

How to Know What Course to Take:
1.   Request a credit or non-credit catalog from your local community college or school district. If you are a displaced homemaker, some colleges have special classes just for you. Often they are free or the fee is on a sliding scale based on your ability to pay.
2.   Look through the business courses and see what interests you. If you are proficient in the basic Microsoft Office programs, you may want to explore a class on finance or classes for starting a business. These are

generally less enticing than the more creative courses, such as cooking and decorating, but the knowledge you gain will be invaluable over time. Use your creativity in implementing new strategies to solve problems at work.

3.   If business does not interest you, you may want to take courses on something you love. Reread some of the lists you've made in doing the exercises in previous chapters; this will help you decide.

4.   Contact the teaching program and ask for a list of who is teaching the courses. Ask about the professors' backgrounds. Ask if the teacher has taught before and if the school or the teacher defines the curriculum of the course(s) you choose to take. A proven curriculum that has been evaluated by former students is important. Ask what kind of feedback the teacher has received.

5.   When the class begins, ask lots of questions. This is your one chance to get the knowledge you need. Make it count.

Ellie's Story

Ellie Peterson grew up in a traditional Catholic family and at sixteen while her friends were picking out prom dresses, she became pregnant. Ellie finished high school and performed clerical work to support the family. She married the father of her child and by the age of twenty-two had a total of three children. The stress of being young parents continued to build and at twenty-three Ellie was divorced. Then she worked in a delicatessen and was the primary provider for her children.

"Taking care of my family was overwhelming," she explained. "But my biggest personal challenges were my negative thought patterns and consequently my own poor self-image."

Stress was commonplace in her life. Ellie had become addicted to cigarettes as a coping mechanism for her mounting anxiety. She began taking aerobic classes and was committed to abandoning the habit. She figured if she became an instructor she'd have to stop smoking in order to keep up with the rigor of her life. But even earning a certification as an aerobics instructor did not help Ellie kick the habit. Eventually, she began seeing a counselor and slowly learned how affirmations such as "I will succeed" could change her thought process.

Ellie realized that she carried incredible guilt about having become pregnant as a teenager and divorced with three children before the age of twenty-three. She thought she would remarry. However, when the opportunity did not present itself, she accepted that she would need to continue to be the sole breadwinner for her family. "Ellie from the deli", as she was fondly called, was making $5.60 an hour while working thirty hours a week and earning $7.00 an hour teaching aerobics classes on the side. In order to be a success, Ellie realized that she needed to change her mindset and her strategy. She decided to go to college. Because of her low income, she qualified for grants and low interest loans to help defer the cost. At the age of thirty-six, she graduated with a degree in business administration with minors in marketing and communications.

As part of a college assignment, Ellie created a business plan for aerobic tapes with a twist: positive affirmations laced into the workout. But she did not have the money, mind-set or emotional support to bring this to market. She instead worked in corporate America as a project manager in information technology and other positions for the next eleven years.

After her children had all moved from home Ellie decided to resurrect her affirming aerobics concept. She had remarried at this point and her husband encouraged her to create a promotional tape. Still she was not sure how to market it. She began taking non-credit classes at Women Venture and asked her colleagues to critique the tape and make recommendations for improving upon it. From there she went on to produce a book and defined her market as health clinicians.

"I continue to live in the moment and release the past and future," she said.

Today Ellie's Meditative Movements is a popular holistic workout program that integrates positive affirmations with Yoga flexibility, balance, strengthening and cardio movements.

"Explore what is out there," Ellie recommends.

Remember: Make every moment of your life precious. Take steps to learn a new way of thinking or a new skill that will create results.

Exercise #24
From Rule No. 24: Don't Go to the Mall—
Go to Computer and Other Classes

The Get Going Quiz
(Take this quiz periodically to update your Educational and Career Plan)

Assessment of Current Career Situation
What is my current personal situation and priorities? For example, priorities may include but not be limited to: income, benefits (e.g., health care, retirement, etc.), child care or eldercare responsibilities, geographic location or work hours.

Identify Educational Interests
1. Which of your personal priorities are being neglected or subjugated as a result of your current situation?

2. What amount of your time outside of the home or office are you willing or able to commit to your career (e.g., self-training, reading industry materials, attending career seminars, etc.)?

3. Do you have any physical or geographical limitations or health considerations to factor into your career choices?

4. What sort of work interests you? What sort of work do you enjoy?

5. Is there a specific employer or position that interests you? Do they pay for professional development or continued college education?

6. Is self-employment your goal? If so, what sort of self-employment situation interests you? Consulting? A business outside the home? A home-based business? Freelancing? Internet-based business? Where can you learn about this?

Brainstorming Without Limits
1. What do you currently do for fun? (If nothing then you need to make a change.)

2. Who are the people you admire? (And notice what they do.)

3. What were your proudest accomplishments at any age? (Your "shining" moments.)

4. What have you always wanted to try?

Chapter Twenty-Five

Rule No. 25

When Everything is Negotiable

Everybody Wins

Before you enter into a conversation with your boss, fellow employees or customers, ask yourself two things:
1. What is it that I want to get out of this conversation?
2. What is it that the other person wants from the conversation?

This becomes especially important when you find yourself in a contentious situation where emotions are high.

Do you want to make the other person feel like an idiot? Or do you want to get what you want? In order to get what you want does the other person have to lose? Can both parties be winners?

Practice putting the emotions aside—it is crucial. When you're in a heated discussion and the other person engages you in a confrontation, think before you speak. If this is hard for you, practice forcing yourself to count to ten before you allow yourself to open your mouth. Once you can clear frustrated energy out of the way, you will say something more relevant and less combative. The other person will be more apt to listen and then negotiate with you, creating a better outcome for both sides.

Negotiating is the process by which two or more parties with different needs and goals work to find a mutually acceptable solution to an issue. The negotiation itself is a careful exploration of your position and the other person's position, with the goal of finding a proper compromise. Everyone is a winner in this process. It is an interpersonal method, influenced by each party's skills, attitudes and style. Often people find the process of negotiating unpleasant, because it implies conflict. Negotiating need not be characterized by bad feelings or angry behavior. It is an art practiced by virtually everyone; it is a craft practiced by few. Understanding and practicing the process allows you to manage your negotiations with confidence.

Most negotiations are repeat performances. We tend to deal with the same fellow employees, suppliers, clients, directors, managers, etc., repeatedly over the same issues. It is important to recognize and give proper weight to the context in which a negotiation is taking place; if it is within an on-going relationship, the significance of that relationship must be considered. Can the relationship be repaired before the crucial issues need to be addressed? Can you have an informal meeting just to discuss building a better relationship? Can you discuss what you agree on and ask them WHY they feel so strongly about their position on which you do not agree?

For many decision-makers, annual obligations like business plan reviews and budget approvals tend to coincide with increased levels of stress and anxiety. We are well-prepared for the matters at hand that need to be decided. It's the process, however, that tends to be quite unsettling. It can be troublesome if stressed relationships and personal agendas get in the way of developing and achieving long-range cooperative goals for a mutual good.

Here is a simple strategy that will help you negotiate better solutions to your conflicts. It is called "the Four Fs of Negotiating." This strategy works in any situation where you need to negotiate a solution to a problem when two people do not agree.

The Four Fs of Negotiating:
I understand how you *Feel*.
I *Felt* the same way until I *Found* out the *Facts*.

First, allow me to put this into context demonstrating a scenario in which I try to negotiate a curfew with one of my teenage children.

Me: Why do you want to stay out until 2:00 in the morning?
Child: Why can't I?
Me: Please tell me what you need to do between midnight and two o'clock that you can't do before midnight?
Child: You don't understand.

Me: I want to understand. Please help me understand. What is it that you want during those hours that can't happen before then?

Child: Everyone else is allowed out and I'd be the only one who would have to come home. I am old enough to stay out with my friends at somebody's house watching television. It's not like I would be alone in someplace that wasn't safe.

Me: Now I understand how you *Feel*. I remember what it was like when I was in high school.

Child: Things are different than when you were young, Mom.

Me: (Ouch!) I remember driving around in my friend Mary Cath's car. We'd ride past all the places where the boys hung out. One night, a really strange guy almost opened one of our doors and got in the car with us. It really freaked us out. Nobody was on the street to help us. It was really late.

Child: Grammie let you cruise?

Me: Not exactly. We always wanted to hang out on the corner with all the cool kids, but our parents would have killed us. So we circled the neighborhood like a posse. Today an evening doing that might cost ten dollars in gas.

Child: *Laughter.* What did you tell Grammie you were doing?

Me: Um, I don't remember. The point I am trying to make is that I now understand that you are not doing anything troublesome. But Mary Cath and I *Felt* we weren't either. Regardless, the *Fact* is that something bad still happened in the early morning hours when no one was around to help us.

Child: You always think everyone is getting in trouble.

Me: I only care that you don't get hurt. I'll make you a deal. Let's set the curfew at 12:30 for two weeks. If you make that, we'll take it to 1:00.

Child: *Rolling eyes.* Okay.

Now let's try this scenario involving the salary negotiations on a job interview.

Me: I am very excited about the opportunity to work for Shore Company and would like to discuss the salary if that is okay with you.

Employer: Certainly. What are your questions?

Me: Do you perceive that I am at the mid or senior level of the job requirements?

Employer: I'd say you are at the mid-level.

Me: Can you tell me why you feel that way?

Employer: Certainly. You have only five years of professional sales experience. And you do not have a four-year degree.

Me: Thank you for your honesty on that. I certainly understand. It is difficult to rate someone's potential when you don't know them at all. Their track record is the only measurable tool of comparison that you have. (I understand how you *Feel*. I *Felt* the same way.)

Employer: Exactly.

Me: Bill, I apologize if I didn't explain this earlier, but is it relative that I was the highest earning sales professional in the three years I was with my last company, earning a $20,000 bonus after just ten months with the company? I actually won a trip to Aruba too. Only the best sales people in each region were invited. When I got back my sales manager made me a regional manager of a piece of her territory where I increased her sales 26 percent the next year. (The *Facts*.)

Employer: Is that so?

Me: Yes I do understand that it is risky hiring someone you don't know. Let me take away some of that risk by showing you this letter of recommendation from that regional sales manager.

Employer: Hmm.

Me: Bill, do you have employees with four-year degrees who are under-performing?

Employer: Yes.

Me: If they went back to college, would it help them be better sales people?

Employer: No.

Me: If your top performers went back to school would it help them be better sales people?

Employer: Probably not. I'd rather have them prospecting.

Me: (Pause.)

Employer: I see your point. I'll place you at the high end of the pay grade.

Me: Thank you, Bill!

For a negotiation to be successful, both parties should feel positive about the negotiation once it's over. This helps you keep good working relationships afterwards. Displays of emotion are clearly inappropriate, because they undermine the rational basis of the negotiation and because they bring in a manipulative aspect to the scenario. People know when they are being manipulated. They feel intimidated and want to escape, which closes the door on the negotiation process.

Rule Break: Don't look at negotiations as win-lose propositions. See them as a win-win. Take the lead at driving the course to a winning destination for both of you.

Five Steps to Gain the Edge in Negotiations:

1. **Separate the people from the problem.** When emotions are high, it is hard to detach from the moment. Additionally, it is hard to detach the individual involved from the message. If sentiments have escalated it is important to pause and collect your thoughts so that you may respond before you react rashly. To diffuse the perception of two parties entering in a conflict against each other, position yourself on the same side of the table as the other party. It shouldn't be "us" against "them" on a battlefield. It should be "we" against an outside enemy.

2. **Prioritize the other person's interests to better understand his or her position.** A classic story to illustrate this describes two sisters fighting over the only orange in the kitchen. Each sister insists she must have no less than the entire orange. Each girl is asked in private why she can't share the orange. One explains she wants to drink the juice; the other wants to use the rind to cook a pudding. *What* each sister really wants is her *position; why* she wants it is her *interest*. In this case, the simple solution is to give the rind to the cook after the juice has been squeezed for the thirsty sister, thus meeting the interests of both. Ask the other party WHY he or she wants what the person wants. This will give you the root cause of his or her *interest* and move them away from the other person's *position*. A solution might be obvious once you understand what is driving the person's behavior. Continuing to ask "WHY" will get at the root cause of all problems.

3. **Consider the best alternative.** If you do not reach an agreement with the other party, does that leave you better or worse than before? What is the worst case scenario that will leave you and the other party better off than before the negotiation? If someone offers you $300 to speak at a conference and you generally charge $1,800 are you better

off not doing the conference or taking a smaller amount of money for the opportunity to present in front of other potential clients? What would the best alternative amount be?

4. **When in doubt, just listen.** If one party is highly emotional, keeping quiet after he or she finishes speaking can be quite unsettling to the person. Most people are troubled by silence in the midst of a heated discussion. Silence is very effective, because it is viewed as a quiet disapproval. When met with silence, people have modified their previous statements to make them more palatable. Detach from the emotion of the moment and just listen.

5. **Pursue integrity.** If all the participants view the process as fair and balanced, they are more likely to take it seriously and "buy into" its result. To be considered successful, an agreement must be sustainable. Parties who walk away from the table grumbling under their breaths may regret their commitments and only honor them grudgingly. If they end up looking for excuses to get out from under unwanted results, the gains will only be short-term.

I have had to negotiate regularly throughout most of my career. Any leader in business finds this a standard part of his or her daily routine; but the most meaningful negotiations I have experienced were in my personal life. I have had countless negotiations with my own children over the use of the car, curfews, chores, course selections, bedtime and taking out the garbage, just to name a few. The most memorable negotiation I ever experienced, however, was about the purchase of my home. And I was not the lead negotiator.

My previous house had recently sold in a Sheriff's Sale just the week prior. The proceeds of the sale were pledged to the debt of my estranged husband's business. The children and I made our goodbyes to the house and knew that a new future lay before us. We were grateful to have found a home in a neighboring suburb within the same school district and that I had a job that could afford it. It was August and the children needed to start school in two weeks so the timing was critical. I was sitting at my desk at Ohio Valley General Hospital one Friday afternoon when I got a call from the real estate agent representing the seller.

"Mary Lee, the seller has decided not to sell the house."

I couldn't believe what he said. "What?"

"I can't tell you how sorry I am." He knew my situation and I believed him. "There is a loophole in the agreement that allows him to do so."

Loophole? When were the loopholes going to start looping in my direction? I thought. I sighed, thanked him for the information, hung up the phone and just stared at it as if surely it would ring back and someone would tell me this was all a bad joke.

The phone did not ring. My assistant could see by my shocked expression and dazed look that something was wrong and I told her what had happened.

"You need to go home," she said. "Go home. We'll be fine here."

I was numb as I made my way to my car and began the drive home on the highway shaking. I walked into the kitchen of the house I had to move out of and give away in two weeks to find that none of my children was home. In the heat of the summer sun they had certainly gone to the neighborhood pool for relief. So, knowing that my friends were probably there, too, I put on my swimsuit and joined them.

"What are you doing here in the middle of the day?" my friends asked.

I just shook my head and slumped down on a lounge chair.

They hovered around. "What is it?"

"You won't believe it."

"What?"

I told them what happened. I could have been looking in the mirror. Their mouths hung open. They had been with me every step of the way and understood the scope of the trials the children and I had suffered.

"You've got to be kidding," they said.

"I'm not." None of us could believe after everything that had happened, another barricade had just been erected in our path.

In times of adversity, you find out who your friends are.

"Well, we'll just have to solve this problem together," said my friend Mary Pat, who went from one cluster of people to another around the pool deck asking if anyone knew of a house that was coming up for sale but had not yet gone on the market. "You need a good deal on a house and there is no room for a real estate commission."

Within thirty minutes, she had networked with enough people to gain a list of three potential houses. "Put on your cover-up," she said. "We're knocking on doors."

I sat up straight. "We can't do that!"

"Sure we can," she responded. "We're not going to sit around here and get down about this."

Here I was, the professional fundraiser afraid to make cold calls. "Are you sure?"

"Get in the car."

The first house was too small so we just drove by. Whew! Nobody was home at the second house, which drew another sigh of relief as I couldn't believe that I was one of two girls in bikinis and wraps knocking on doors in our own neighborhood.

Mary Pat knocked on the door of the third house and a blonde woman with a kind face answered.

"I am Mary Pat from down the street and this is my friend Mary Lee and she just found out today that the house that she was buying is no longer for sale. She has four kids who need to start school in two weeks. We heard that your house might be coming on the market and thought we'd see if you were interested in selling it?" She took a deep breath after getting that out. I was shrinking behind her.

"As a matter of fact I have a sales agreement on the table," the woman said.

"Oh, don't sign that yet," said Mary Pat, waving her hands. "Can we come in and take a look around?"

I cringed. Had my friend really asked a stranger if we could come into her house?

"Sure, come on in," the woman said.

We fell in love with the house instantly and developed an immediate friendship with its owner, but price was an issue.

"I am approved for a mortgage at a certain amount and can buy the house right away," I said. "But I can't go any higher."

"You need this house," the woman told me and helped negotiate the price on my behalf with her husband. You see who your angels are.

This kind soul developed an instant bond with us and became our guest at the pool for the rest of the weekend and on a regular basis for the two weeks before she moved away.

She even allowed me to move our belongings into the home before the closing so that the children were able to join their friends at their old school on the first day.

Remember: Negotiate deals that leave everyone a winner. Recognize who your angels are and celebrate the good things in your life.

Exercise #25
From Rule No. 25: When Everything is Negotiable
Everybody Wins

Small Acts of Kindness

Below is a list of kind things you might say or do for someone. Next to each one put the name of a person you know who might be touched by this act or kind words. If you can't think of an individual, list the name of an organization that this act might serve. You might even fill these in as you go along.

Act of Kindness	Recipient of this Act of Kindness	Date
1. Recommend a good book to someone. Lend it to them if you own it.		
2. Give someone a homemade gift.		
3. Forgive someone when they apologize.		
4. Forgive someone who hasn't apologized.		
5. Call your cousins.		
6. Tell someone: "You make it look easy."		
7. Be a mentor or coach to someone.		
8. Forgive a loan.		
9. Send a copy of an old photograph to a childhood friend.		
10. Tell someone: "You are very good at that."		
11. Do a household chore that is usually done by someone else in the family.		
12. Tell someone: "Keep working on it, you're getting better.		
13. Tell someone, "I believe in you."		
14. Ask someone if they need you to pick up anything while you're out shopping.		
15. Ask a child to play a board game.		

Act of Kindness	Recipient of this Act of Kindness	Date
16. Bake a cake for a neighbor.		
17. Ask an elderly person to tell you about the good old days.		
18. Tell someone: "You are doing an amazing job."		
19. Bring cookies to work.		
20. Tell a cashier to have a nice day.		
21. Ask an older person for his or her advice.		
22. Tell someone: "You are incredible."		
23. Treat someone to a movie.		
24. Tell someone: "Couldn't have done it better myself."		
25. Leave a thank-you note for the cleaning staff at work.		

Afterword

One piece of advice that I have found to be more worthwhile than any other words of wisdom I've ever received is, "Say only kind things about people." If you are managing people, customer needs or projects and you expect people to work with the same ethic as you do, you may meet with disappointment if your expectations are high. Be supportive. If you are an achiever or an entrepreneur, you may find it difficult to repeatedly concentrate on only fine qualities in people since you will find that many people do not possess the drive or work ethic that you do. Be patient and nurturing with yourself and others. It will come.

The reason it is important to say only good things about others is that when you point out the bad things that people do, they essentially tune you out, because what you are saying is painful for them to admit. They will not only tune you out, but also find fault with you so that they can justify tuning you out. "She's mean and unrealistic anyway." You have lost their respect. It's a horrible place to be if you need to inspire them to work with you toward a goal.

Never point out mistakes or shortcomings in a crisis—support people in a crisis. Chances are that they are beating themselves up enough already. You need not add to the abuse. If people who report to you have made a mistake, help them figure out what they can do next time to avoid such mistakes. Work with them. Recognize that you know they are conscientious workers. Praise them for something specific they do well. I often admit to a colleague that I could have made the same mistake and offer whatever safeguards I might put in place so as to best catch the mistake before it actually occurs. By humanizing the mistake as something anyone could have done, it eases his or her embarrassment. Then you have earned the colleague's respect. Help people define processes they can put into place to keep mistakes from happening again. Being punitive never gets you anything but being the topic of lunchtime critique.

People around you will admire your grace if you do not make them feel worse than they already do when they have made mistakes. They will respect you if you help them find ways not to make these mistakes again. And they will support whatever you are working toward if you do all of these things consistently and support their efforts while reminding them along the way of how much you value their work.

The number one rule to remember about your boss: ALWAYS make your boss look good. Do everything you can to support your boss, because he or she is the most important person in making your climb up the ladder short. Your boss needs to be able to count on you. You want to be his go-to person. You want to be the one she comes to when she needs to hear the truth. You will earn that status in her eyes by being consistent, positive and supportive.

Being supportive when colleagues make mistakes or pointing out their strengths is a sure way to make people want to be around you. Another way to do this is through humor. I love to laugh. If you can make people laugh, they will surely want to be around you. Not everyone is a comedian. And please do not try to be funny if you are not naturally comedic. However, in an effort to further humanize yourself to the people whom you work for, with and around, as well as your customers, poke fun only at yourself—not others.

Many of the comedians on television programs make people laugh by making fun of other people. That is humor at someone else's expense and is not as innovative as something really funny. Comedians who use this technique seem to come and go.

When you think of things that are truly funny and not at someone else's expense, they generally are things that are "Aha! moments." These "Aha! moments" are things you hear and say, "Aha! I remember that." Jerry Seinfeld is a traditional "Aha! moment" comedian. He need not use profanity or mockery to get a laugh. He just talks about real life. That is why he has been popular for such a long time. Your own life should give you enough material to keep people laughing for a lifetime.

Humor is a wonderful asset to draw upon in a difficult situation. A laugh, even a simple smile, can lift anyone from a low moment. It is not easy to find "Aha! moments" when you feel overwhelmed, but if you can do so you will begin to see that despair is only a temporary state of mind. Profound sadness might be how you feel right now, but not forever.

Although my children endured much despair in their lives, their greatest tribulation came when they were all in high school and middle school. Their father had become very sick and a year later he lost his battle with cancer and passed away. It was devastating. The children had already been through more trauma in their short lives than anyone should have to undergo. They had already suffered their parents' malevolent divorce, lost their home, had to switch schools, survived on public assistance and not had their mother available because she was constantly working. They had been through a great deal of turmoil on a daily basis; now there was none. I know that life tests the strength of our grit and the roots of our faith, but this new trial was one that I felt we needed help to endure. In doing so we sought the help of the Highmark Caring Place, a two-month grief support program for children and their families.

In the beginning, the children were very reluctant to go to the program. Their pain was difficult enough to bear. They didn't want to have to *talk* about their pain. But the program wasn't intrusive. The children talked about what they wanted to talk about in a group of their peers. They made craft projects—and they ate pizza.

We learned incidentally that everyone grieves differently, especially children. Grief isn't a process that you study, work your way through and eventually get awarded peace of mind. It is a journey that lasts a lifetime. Some days may be good; some are not. As time goes by, the good days outnumber the bad. The bad days are part of the journey. It is okay to have bad days. Embrace them as how you feel today—it doesn't mean you will feel that way tomorrow.

Once the children saw that other children their own ages were experiencing similar pain and suffering, they did not feel so alone or isolated. We went home one night and got out all the old pictures of their father and remembered some of the laughs we all shared together. These photos still adorn our home today as do the laughs we share when we remember funny things he said or did. Through this program, our family was able to rediscover our "Aha! moments." Everyone was able to laugh again.

At the end of the Highmark Caring Place program we were asked to be the guest speakers at the program's annual volunteer recognition dinner.

When I said we would do this, I felt that we needed to give back, because the program was so helpful to my children and their healing process. I thought the speech was supposed to be in front of a small group of people. It ended up being for more than 200 people. I couldn't imagine what I would say that would interest them about our experience. I decided to talk honestly about what we had learned while lacing through the speech the truth of what it was like to engage four teenagers to do anything. I could have thanked the volunteers with a lot of flowery language and told them how much my four children looked forward to the program. Instead, I showed them a sincere look at our experience. The audience seemed to be able to relate to it. The frank specifics of our teenage household life made them laugh. It was a difficult subject. We needed to lighten it up. Poking fun at ourselves helped to do that.

I explained that our ride down to the first meeting was similar to our church experience. I think they expected me to say that my children were inspired to be there but instead I told them the truth. On the ride to that first meeting, my children repeatedly told me, "I can't believe you're making us do this. Nobody else's mother makes them do this." I told them how my thirteen-year-old son flipped backwards over the chairs in the lobby while the director told him, "Chairs are for sitting." Then I told them how my children started asking if we could stop for coffee after the meetings on a regular basis, how I had to learn to pronounce the coffee flavors and how we started talking again over those coffee moments after what had been an excruciatingly painful episode in our lives. To bring it all full circle, I thanked the volunteers for opening their arms to a safe place for us to come and return to being ourselves. Maria and Brianna shared with the audience how being at the Caring Place felt like home, a place where they could regularly go and just be themselves with other young people who understood what they were going through.

Just being your honest self is enough to keep anyone interested in what you have to say. And the candid truth without pretense is sometimes what is the most engaging. Poke honest fun at yourself. You have a lifetime of material.

Rule Break: While saying only kind things of others is a mark of character, do not disregard that there are times when others do things that leave no room for admiration. At those times, do not look the other way and ignore the truth of the situation. Make decisions that are appropriate for you. Those decisions may be painful. You need not engage in confrontation for the sake of confrontation. Engage in a discussion only for the purpose of fact finding. Gather facts then make the best decision you can make for yourself without allowing emotion to get in the way. Emotional discussions end up leading to rides down the chute. In a confrontational situation, pause, take a breath and then respond. Don't immediately react. You'll say something you'll regret.

Characteristics of Good Praise:

1. Compliment something she did that you did not ask her to do. "Nice work noticing that the addresses in that list had not been updated and checking them against the other database before the mailing."
2. Be specific on what you compliment him. Not just, "Good job." More like, "Nice work escorting that customer to the shipping dock when you could have just pointed in that direction."
3. Give simple gestures of thanks—warm cookies, simple holiday decorations for desks, lunch out, etc.
4. From time to time, write personal notes of thanks and send them home.
5. Recognize him or her publicly at a meeting for good work.

Examples of Outstanding Praise: (Don't be afraid to be personal. Good praise is personal.)

1. I trust you.
2. You mean a lot to me and this team.
3. You care.
4. You are a joy.
5. I am proud of you.
6. I like you.
7. You're a winner.
8. Phenomenal work!
9. Exceptional performance.
10. You are responsible.
11. What an imagination.
12. What a good listener.
13. You're important.
14. You belong.
15. You brighten my day.

In the Words of Others Who Did It

As I interviewed the vast array of talent featured in this book who were gracious enough to share their experiences for the purpose of guiding others, I found as I concluded their section that there was extremely valuable insight that had not fit in. Nonetheless, their additional advice is too important not to include. Here are some words of wisdom on leadership, self doubt, challenge, success, goals and inspiration from these giving souls. Allow these messages to enlighten you on your journey. And notice some common themes in their words.

Kellyann Dinoff, Principal, Sonance Communications
"Take a look at what made you happy in your career and seek out those qualities in your next position."

Regarding what contributed to her success: "Great support from my friends, family, past co-workers and managers was important. That, and sticking to what I know and love best. It is easier to put in hours when you're passionate about what you're doing."

Regarding common traits in people who have achieved success amidst overwhelming challenge: "Plain and simple—they love what they do and seek out whatever means necessary to keep doing it."

"Owning your own business is not as scary as it sounds. It's the most secure and fulfilling job I ever had."

Victoria Star, Founder, Discovery Map International

"There is a part of me that wants to believe you can be successful without the pain. But when you really work hard for something, winning is so much sweeter. Is it the destination or is it really the journey? I'm still on the journey....You have to be very thick-skinned, you need to make sacrifices, you have to take risks and you have to be willing to fail in order to succeed. That's a tall order.

"No matter what, I just refused to give up. I always believed that where there was a will there was a way. And if I couldn't see the way, I needed to ask for directions, and I did.

"Seek out mentors and/or advisors who have proven experience. The Small Business Administration has a mentors program that is free and that's a good place to start.

"Don't isolate yourself. Become and stay active in your community.

"Stay healthy and fit; take time to take care of yourself. You are your most valuable asset.

"I've always been inspired by individuals who challenge convention, who motivate me to think outside the box—women who beat the odds.

"A great company fills a need instead of manufacturing one. A great company delivers on its promises, and then some. A great company delivers a quality product, takes care of its customers and has fun in the process. Southwest Airlines is a great company. The Body Shop is a great company. Discovery Map is on its way to becoming a great company."

Ruth Kuttler, Director, WebPuzzleMaster, LLC

"I was like a square peg in a round hole. When it got painful enough, I changed jobs or went back to school to get another degree in my field. After seven years in school and a post-master's degree with twenty-five years' experience in health care, I finally came to understand that it was never going to work for me. Finally my employer gave me a gift and laid me off.

"For the first time in my life, I felt empowered to do whatever it took to design the life I really wanted. I vowed to let go of self-limiting beliefs and fears. I distanced myself from non-supportive people. I started to read personal development books and attend personal development seminars.

"Everything happens as it is supposed to. We are all presented with opportunities to learn, discover and grow. I think that I needed to experience true unhappiness to learn about happiness. I needed to experience mediocrity to learn about living with passion. I don't believe I would have changed those experiences.

"I believe that whatever we believe and think about, we attract into our lives. I make a point of visualizing what I want every day.

"Successful people see opportunity where others see no way out. They don't dwell on mistakes, live in the past, blame others or take failure personally. They learn from adversity and move on. Another quality of successful people is that they take personal responsibility for what happens to them.

"Good leaders solicit input from their employees and value their opinions. Effective leadership is not about ego. It is helping somebody become the best they can be. Whether you are starting your life over in your own business or working for somebody else—don't be in a stifling environment. Don't be complacent to sit back and do a menial job in the easiest way possible. Make it into the best opportunity it can be. If you see something that can be done better, do whatever you can to make it better.

"There are five keys to success. 1) Passion: Your health, your career and every aspect of your life has to come from a place of passion. If you don't know what to do, give yourself the opportunity to experience life to its fullest. 2) Intention: You have to have set an intention of 100 percent. You can't wait for your family to say it's okay or to have the money in the bank. You say, 'I am going to change my life. I am not sure how but somehow it is going to happen.' 3) Empowerment: Commit to doing something today that will support your transition—books, courses, school and working on yourself. 4) Adversity: Understand that if things do not work out it does not make you a failure. You made a mistake and have learned a valuable lesson from it. Mistakes are your friends and teach and guide you to be stronger. 5) Persistence: Get a mentor. Get a business coach. Don't throw in the towel, because the first thing you attempted did not work out."

Judy Briggs, Franchise Partner, 1-800-GOT-JUNK?
"Have confidence in your ability and never let anyone tell you you're crazy. If you are passionate about what you want to do then there is nothing to stop you. The only one to stop you is you.

"Failure is not an option."

Regarding common traits in people who have achieved success amidst overwhelming challenge: "They have a positive attitude. The people they surround themselves with have it, too. Passion—you can see it in people's eyes—it's like a fire. They have a thirst for achievement."

Kevin Sullivan, Chief Marketing Officer, Fisher & Phillips, LLP
"In my current position I have to be a generalist serving many masters.

"I never doubted that I would succeed.

"At first, being fired felt humiliating. But I kept saying that I would not let it get me down and that I would come back. I knew I had what it takes to succeed in something other than television.

"If faced with challenge don't panic. Stay calm. Become very focused on what you want to do then figure out a plan to get there. Finding a new career is a full-time job and you should treat it as such. Also, be willing to take interim jobs so that you can pay the bills while you renew your career. In between television and my first corporate marketing job I spent six months as assistant manager of a fast-food restaurant. That was the most eye-opening experience of my life!

"Stay upbeat. Even when you are down and you think things can't get worse, don't show it on the outside. People do not gravitate to people who are depressed. If you maintain a positive attitude people will respond to you in a positive way."

Regarding common traits in people who have achieved success amidst overwhelming challenge: "These people have the ability to remain calm while everything around them seems chaotic. They are able to stay focused on a goal and are willing to sacrifice and work hard to achieve a goal. These people also believe in themselves. They know instinctively what to do and what not to do. Even when they are down they don't forget other people. They do not wallow in self-pity. If you meet one of these people for the first time and you are unaware they are experiencing a stressful challenge, you won't be able to detect it."

Drew J. Stevens Ph.D., President, Stevens Consulting Group
"Life is too short and you need to live your life doing something that you are passionate about.

"Individuals who meet overwhelming challenges have three things: 1) Risk: They are not fearful and meet it head-on. 2) Focus: Successful entrepreneurs have a single focus. They know what they want and remain focused on the goal. 3) Failure: Successful people are not afraid to fail. Failure is education and if you are not failing you are not learning.

"Constantly educate yourself. Nobody can take it away.

"Thomas Edison said, 'I have not failed. I've just found 10,000 ways that won't work.' Failure is education. Look at it as an opportunity to take it to another level.

"If you are thinking of running a business, go for it. My mother-in-law passed away at sixty-one. At the time she was double my age. I remember thinking that half of my life could be over and I was tired of living unhappily and being someone else's slave.

"I resisted mentors early on and it was a mistake. You need a support mechanism.

"When you lack funds you do your best thinking.

"I attribute where I am to three things: 1) Goals were my GPS from day one. 2) I have educated myself along the way. I ask questions. 3) I convey a message. Realize what your assets are and tell people."

Tawnya Sutherland, Founder, VAnetworking.com

"Once I knew success was in my own hands, the rest was easy...just wake up and do it each day.

"Finding enough time in the day is usually my biggest concern. There are so many things that need to be done to make this business successful. Being a perfectionist hasn't helped me any and probably has held me back.

"Success is a mind-set. Everything has challenges, that is just the journey.

"I have three 'P's for success. Persistence—to never give up and keep pushing through your business plan no matter what obstacles stand in your way. Passion—and solid desire to reach the vision you have for you and your business. Populace—networking with like-minded people.

"Great companies listen to what their customers want and give it to them.

"I would have delegated more in the beginning instead of trying to do it all myself."

Regarding common traits in people who have achieved success amidst overwhelming challenge: "They tend to be tenacious, risk takers, givers and opportunists."

Lisa Stancati, Assistant General Counsel, ESPN

"Conquering challenges and adversity is the best and quickest way to develop authentic self-confidence, which no one can ever take away from you.

"A great company is defined by leadership manifested through character, integrity and vision.

"If you stay committed to something long enough, it will turn. You must persevere."

Maryann Karinch, Author/Agent, The Rudy Agency
"My goals for the future are to live with gratitude and passion.

"Integrity defines a great company.

"You have to be logical and willing to fail and realize that failure is learning steps. This doesn't mean that the setback buries you. Sometimes when you run down the road, you step in a hole.

"You have to have constant passion and be very excited about what you're doing. Don't be an actress who never goes on an audition. Some people make a plan. Winners DO the plan.

"Hard times are important.

"Get yourself a mentor. Model yourself after someone you admire. Study the person. That person can be from afar. If you are going to do things right you need a role model. You need to follow in the steps of someone who knows what he or she is doing."

Ellie Peterson, Inspirer, Meditative Movements
"My advice is that individuals need to listen and honor themselves. Change takes time, so I have found I need to forgive myself when I fall short of my intentions and continue to persevere with the affirmations and movements on a daily basis so I can live confidently and with gentle peace.

"I surround myself with individuals who are living life and can share their experiences and journeys with me. For me it's fun to feel that connection.

"Be open to opportunities.

"Ask questions.

"Share the honesty of who you are."

Conclusion

You have everything you need to be a success. With dedication, character and access to mentors and good information you will succeed. Know that and never doubt it. When things don't seem to be going your way, take a step up the ladder and look down on your life from another angle. Are you failing early and perhaps need to take another route? Are you praying for the wrong thing? Is the journey just a little longer than you originally thought? Are you fearless, not reckless? Can you be patient?

In the early phase of my starting over years I spent a lot of time feeling worried and desperate. I can tell you with absolute certainty that all of that worry and desperation did not do one thing to help me. They only dragged me further away from where I wanted to be.

During that time when I was not sure how I would feed my children or if they would ever be able to go to college or if I would ever own my own home again, I was telling myself a lot of "can'ts". "I can't let faith carry me because I am not sure where I am going to live and how I will pay the bills. I can't relax because I have so much to do. I can't trust that my children will be okay, because I am not sure how we will survive."

All of those "can'ts" turned into "won'ts". I did not initially have great faith. I was not able to relax. I did not trust that my own abilities could carry my family.

Thankfully, while I was obsessing over my fears, I did not waiver on my goals. I pursued a certification of which the process taught me far more than the certificate could ever mean. I was able to secure better press coverage for my public relations clients than they had ever seen. I broke all trade show attendance records for the association I was directing. I raised more money than the institutions for which I worked had ever raised.

Eventually in doing these things, I began to realize that if I was able to accomplish these outstanding triumphs, why should I worry so much about the future. My faith became stronger. My trust in myself skyrocketed. I accepted that as long as I was alive, God had already given me the ability to right my own destiny for good purpose, even if that meant some transitions along the way.

Today I am grateful to have a fine position where I mentor and have colleagues whom I hold as dear as family and my four wonderful children are thriving. My children are indeed my greatest pride. I used to worry that what we went through would negatively affect the children. I found that much of the experience was a blessing in disguise. Today I never regret that I was not able to take my family around the world on vacations or give them the latest car or other electronic device like many of their friends' parents did. On Christmas Day when my children's friends are describing what electronic devices they got for the holidays, we are delivering poinsettia plants to hospital patients.

I have been dedicated to giving my children life lessons that I hope have equipped them to be happy, meaningful and productive members of society while also maintaining sensitivity and respect for others. They make me proud. My two oldest children, Maria and Brianna, are well into their college careers, thriving and leading on their campuses. Both girls acquired partial scholarships to top tier schools. Were they in the top 3 percent of their class, where most students are who achieve these scholarships? No. Instead they had good grades coupled with well-rounded lives complete with 100+ hours of volunteer service, work experience and outstanding leadership activities. Maria chaired President Barack Obama's campaign on her campus and had the opportunity to have him thank her in person when he came there to speak. Brianna leads several leadership development programs on her campus and still volunteers at hospitals and with the underserved. My third child, Andrea, just began college this fall with a partial scholarship as well. Her creative talents and dedication to developing her art skills to teach and counsel others is an inspiration to all of us. She sees through all pretenses and has a common sense that is rivaled by none. My youngest child, Max, is in high school and has a business sense and social savvy that are remarkable for someone his age. I entertain myself by thinking this comes in part from having taken him with me around town to business meetings while he was in his formative preschool years and I couldn't find babysitters.

All of the children have learned to manage their time, work hard and give back. This isn't to say that the hard times did not affect them. Those times affected all of us and often brought out the worst in us. But they did not wear us down. And they did not wear us out. At times, we were angry. At times, we felt fearful and alone. And sometimes we couldn't help but feel that life wasn't fair. Throughout this journey, however, we never lost sight of our dedication to one another and to our own abilities. Over time, anger turned to forgiveness. Fear turned to faith. And fairness became gratefulness for all that we had already been given.

If you endure a life-changing event and still have sensitivity, love and trust in your heart, you have a lot to give the world. So get moving. The world has a lot of needs for those qualities.

NOTES